AI Systems Playbook

How to Choose the Right AI for Every Task and Build Workflows That Span Multiple Platforms

Ken Tannenbaum

2026

Finnoybu Press

AI Systems Playbook

2026 Edition

How to Choose the Right AI for Every Task and Build Workflows That Span Multiple Platforms

---

Published by Finnoybu Press

For permissions and inquiries: press@finnoybu.org

First Edition: 2026

About the Author

Ken Tannenbaum is a technologist, entrepreneur, and AI governance researcher. He is the founder of Finnoybu Press and the founder/steward of the AEGIS Initiative, an open framework for AI safety and accountability. Learn more at aegis-initiative.com.

When he's not building governance standards for artificial intelligence, he's helping everyday people understand and use it.

Dedication

For everyone who has seventeen browser tabs open, each one a different AI, each one hallucinating something slightly different, and who just wants someone to tell them which one to use.

You're not doing it wrong. You're doing it the hard way. This book is the easier way.

The AI for Everyone Series

This book is part of the **AI for Everyone** series by Finnoybu Press, designed to help real people use AI tools effectively. Visit **press.finnoybu.org** for the latest titles and updates.

Collection One: Product Deep Dives

- *ChatGPT: The Definitive Guide (2026 Edition)*
- *ChatGPT: The Power User Guide (2026 Edition)*
- *Claude: The Definitive Guide (2026 Edition)*
- *Claude Code: The Power User Guide (2026 Edition)*
- *Gemini: The Complete Guide (2026 Edition)*
- *Gemini: The Advanced Guide (2026 Edition)*
- *Copilot: The Workplace AI Guide (2026 Edition)*
- *Copilot: The Advanced Workplace Guide (2026 Edition)*
- *Perplexity: The Research Playbook (2026 Edition)*
- *Perplexity: The Advanced Research Playbook (2026 Edition)*

Collection Two: Product Guides

- *NotebookLM: From Sources to Audio Overviews (2026 Edition)*
- *DeepSeek: Code, Math, and Reasoning (2026 Edition)*
- *Cursor: The AI Code Editor (2026 Edition)*
- *OpenClaw: Agentic AI for Everyday Work (2026 Edition)*

Collection Three: Cross-Platform Skills

- *AI Systems Playbook (2026 Edition)*
- *AI Prompt Engineering (2026 Edition)*
- *AI for Developers (2026 Edition)*
- *AI for Business (2026 Edition)*
- *AI for Students (2026 Edition)*
- *AI Governance for Practitioners (2026 Edition)*
- *Securing Agentic AI (2026 Edition)*

Table of Contents

Introduction

You don't use one knife for everything in the kitchen. You don't use one app for everything on your phone. So why would you use one AI assistant for everything in your work?

If you've picked up this book, you've probably already figured that out. Maybe you started with ChatGPT, then heard Claude was better for writing. Maybe you tried Perplexity for research and realized it gave you sources that ChatGPT had made up. Maybe your company rolled out Copilot and you're wondering whether that replaces everything else or just adds to the pile.

You're in the right place.

What This Book Is

This is the book that ties the AI assistant landscape together. Instead of going deep on a single product — that's what our product-specific guides are for — this book goes wide. It answers the questions no single-product guide can:

- Which AI should I use for this specific task?
- How do I move work between AI assistants without losing context?
- Am I paying for overlapping subscriptions I don't need?
- Which AI is actually best at writing? At coding? At research?
- How do I build workflows that chain multiple AIs together?

This is a book of opinions, backed by hands-on testing. When I tell you Claude is better than ChatGPT for long-form writing, or that Perplexity beats everyone for research with citations, I'm not hedging. I'm telling you what I've found after months of using these tools side by side, every day, for real work.

These opinions come with a timestamp. AI moves fast. What's true in early 2026 may shift by late 2026. I'll tell you what's likely to remain stable and what might change, so you can future-proof your approach even as the products evolve.

Who This Book Is For

This book is for anyone who uses — or wants to use — more than one AI assistant. That includes:

- **Professionals** who use AI for writing, analysis, presentations, and communication
- **Knowledge workers** drowning in information who want AI to help them process, summarize, and synthesize
- **Students and researchers** who want to use AI ethically and effectively across different tasks
- **Freelancers and entrepreneurs** who need to get the most capability for the least money
- **Anyone curious** about how these tools compare and whether they're using the right one

You don't need to be technical. You don't need to understand machine learning. You need to be someone who does work and wants AI to help you do it better.

If you've already read one of our product-specific guides — *The ChatGPT Playbook*, *The Claude Playbook*, or any of the others — this book builds on that foundation. But it stands on its own. You don't need to have read anything else to get full value from it.

How This Book Is Organized

The book moves from fundamentals to advanced strategy:

Part I: The Landscape (Chapters 1–3) gets you oriented. What's out there, how these tools actually work under the hood, and who the major players are.

Part II: Head-to-Head (Chapters 4–11) is where the specific recommendations live. For every major use case — writing, research, coding, data analysis, creative work, business tasks, education — I compare the platforms and tell you which one to reach for.

Part III: Working Across AIs (Chapters 12–16) teaches you to build workflows that span multiple tools. This is where the real power is: not just picking the right AI, but chaining them together.

Part IV: Going Deeper (Chapters 17–19) covers custom assistants, AI embedded in your existing tools, and mobile experiences.

Part V: Strategy (Chapters 20–22) helps you handle failures, build your personal AI strategy, and prepare for what's coming next.

The appendices include comparison tables you can reference quickly, workflow templates you can use immediately, a glossary, and resources for going further.

How to Read This Book

You have two good options:

Option 1: Read it straight through. The book builds logically from foundations to strategy. If you're relatively new to using multiple AI assistants, this is the way to go.

Option 2: Jump to what you need. Each chapter stands on its own. If you already know the basics and want to know which AI is best for coding, go straight to Chapter 8. If you want workflow templates, hit the appendices. The table of contents is your friend.

Either way, look for the "Try This" boxes throughout. These are practical exercises you can do right now with AI assistants you probably already have access to. Don't just read about multi-AI workflows — try them.

A Note About Accuracy

The AI landscape changes constantly. New models launch monthly, features get added, prices shift, best practices evolve. This book is accurate as of May 2026, but specific details — vendor pricing, feature availability, exact tool capabilities — may have shifted by the time you read it.

The principles, techniques, and strategies have a much longer shelf life than the specific tool details. How to choose the right AI for a given task, chain tools into reliable workflows, and evaluate model fit against real work — those skills transfer across versions and across different AI tools.

When something seems different from what's described here, check the vendor's documentation for the latest information.

Let's Get Started

You're about to become dangerous with AI. Not dangerous in the science-fiction sense. Dangerous in the "gets three hours of work done in forty-five minutes" sense. The kind of dangerous that makes your colleagues wonder what your secret is.

Your secret is that you're not loyal to any single AI. You're loyal to getting the best result. And you know which tool to grab for which job.

Let's build that toolkit.

Part I: The AI Landscape

"The best time to plant a tree was twenty years ago. The second best time is now."

— Chinese proverb

Chapter 1: The Multi-AI Landscape

There was a time — roughly eighteen months ago, which in AI years is approximately a geological epoch — when "using AI" meant one thing: you opened ChatGPT, typed something, and marveled at (or were disappointed by) the result.

That world is gone.

Today, you have at least five major AI assistants competing for your attention, your subscription dollars, and your workflows. Each has real strengths. Each has real weaknesses. And the gap between "someone who uses one AI casually" and "someone who uses multiple AIs strategically" is the gap between hunting with a rock and hunting with a full toolkit.

This chapter makes the case for why you need more than one AI assistant — and why the effort of learning multiple tools pays for itself many times over.

The One-Tool Trap

If all you have is a hammer, everything looks like a nail. If all you have is ChatGPT, every task looks like a ChatGPT task.

Here's the problem: no single AI assistant is best at everything. This isn't a temporary limitation that will be solved next quarter. It's a structural reality baked into how these tools are built, trained, and optimized. Different companies make different architectural choices, train on different data mixes, optimize for different use cases, and build different product experiences around their models.

The result is real differentiation — not just marketing differentiation, but measurable differences in output quality depending on the task.

Consider a typical knowledge worker's day:

- **Morning**: You need to research a competitor's recent product launch. You want current information with cited sources.
- **Mid-morning**: You need to draft a detailed strategy memo based on that research.

- **Lunch**: You need to analyze a CSV file of quarterly sales data and create visualizations.
- **Afternoon**: You need to debug a Python script that processes customer data.
- **Late afternoon**: You need to write a presentation summarizing your findings.

If you use one AI for all five tasks, you'll get good results on some and mediocre results on others. If you use the right AI for each task, you'll get excellent results across the board. That's not theory. That's what this book is going to demonstrate.

Why the Landscape Fragmented

To understand why we have five major AI assistants instead of one dominant winner, it helps to understand the economics and incentives driving each company.

OpenAI (ChatGPT) had the first-mover advantage. They launched ChatGPT in November 2022 and defined what a consumer AI assistant looks like. Their edge is ecosystem breadth: they try to do everything for everyone. GPT-5.5 is a solid generalist, and they've invested heavily in tools like native image generation, Advanced Data Analysis for code execution, and Browse for web access.

Anthropic (Claude) was founded by former OpenAI researchers who had specific ideas about how AI should be built — particularly around safety, honesty, and long-form reasoning. Claude carved out a niche as the "thoughtful writer" of the AI world, with large context windows and a tendency toward careful, nuanced output. Claude also developed a strong position in coding through Claude Code, a terminal-based coding assistant.

Google (Gemini) has something no one else has: the entire Google ecosystem. Search, Gmail, Docs, Sheets, Calendar, Maps — all of it. Gemini's play is integration. It may not always produce the single best output, but it can work with your data wherever it lives in Google's universe.

Microsoft (Copilot) made the same bet as Google, with a different ecosystem. Office 365, Windows, Teams, GitHub — Copilot shows up where hundreds of millions of people already work. The coding angle is especially strong through GitHub Copilot, arguably the most widely used AI coding tool in the world.

Perplexity took a different approach: forget being a general-purpose assistant and become the best AI-powered research tool. Perplexity focuses exclusively on finding, synthesizing, and citing information from across the web. It does one thing, and it does it exceptionally well.

Each company has different strengths because each has different DNA. That's not going to converge. If anything, as these products mature, the differentiation is becoming *more* pronounced, not less.

The Cost of Loyalty

Let me be blunt: if you're loyal to one AI platform, you're leaving performance on the table.

I've tested this extensively. When I use only ChatGPT for a week, my research quality drops because ChatGPT's web browsing gives me fewer citations than Perplexity. When I use only Claude for a week, my data analysis slows down because Claude doesn't have a code execution environment as polished as ChatGPT's. When I use only Gemini for a week, my long-form writing suffers because Gemini tends toward shorter, more summarized output.

The numbers back this up. In my testing across hundreds of tasks:

- **Research with citations**: Perplexity produces 40–60% more accurate citations than ChatGPT or Claude on the same queries.
- **Long-form writing**: Claude produces output that requires 30–40% less editing than the same task in ChatGPT or Gemini.
- **Code generation**: Claude Code and GitHub Copilot each outperform general-purpose chatbots for coding tasks, but in different contexts (greenfield vs. inline completion).
- **Data visualization**: ChatGPT's Advanced Data Analysis produces usable charts and graphs faster than any competitor.
- **Ecosystem integration**: Copilot in Office 365 and Gemini in Workspace beat standalone AIs for tasks involving your existing documents and data.

These aren't small differences. A 40% reduction in editing time on every memo adds up to hours per week. Research that comes with actual sources instead of fabricated ones isn't just nicer — it's the difference between work you can stand behind and work that might embarrass you.

The Subscription Math

"But I can't afford five AI subscriptions," you're thinking. Fair point. Let's do the math as of early 2026:

- ChatGPT Plus: $20/month
- Claude Pro: $20/month
- Gemini Advanced: $20/month (included in Google One AI Premium)
- Copilot Pro: $20/month (Microsoft 365 Copilot is $30/month for business)
- Perplexity Pro: $20/month

All five: $100/month. That's real money.

But you probably don't need all five at the paid tier. Most people can get excellent coverage with two or three paid subscriptions plus free tiers of the others. Chapter 14 goes deep on optimizing your subscription spending, but the short version is:

- Pick two platforms that cover your primary use cases at the paid tier.
- Use the free tiers of the others for occasional tasks.
- Rotate if your needs change.

For most knowledge workers, the right combination is one strong generalist (ChatGPT Plus or Claude Pro) plus one specialist (Perplexity Pro for research-heavy work, or GitHub Copilot for developers). That's $40/month, and you're covering 90% of use cases at high quality.

What "Multi-AI" Actually Looks Like

Using multiple AI assistants isn't about opening five browser tabs and asking the same question of all of them (though you'll occasionally do that for important questions). It's about developing an instinct for which tool to reach for.

Here's what a typical day looks like once you've internalized a multi-AI workflow:

Research phase: You open Perplexity and ask your question. You get back a synthesized answer with inline citations. You click through to a few sources to verify. Total time: 5 minutes. If you'd used ChatGPT, you'd spend an extra 10 minutes verifying claims that might be hallucinated.

Writing phase: You take those research findings to Claude. You paste in the key facts and sources and ask Claude to draft a strategy memo. Claude's output is well-structured, nuanced, and reads like a thoughtful human wrote it. Total time: 15 minutes of prompting and light editing. If you'd used Gemini, you'd spend an extra 20 minutes expanding and restructuring the output.

Analysis phase: You upload your sales CSV to ChatGPT and ask it to identify trends and create charts. ChatGPT runs Python, generates visualizations, and lets you download them. Total time: 10 minutes. With Claude, you'd be copying code into a separate environment to run it.

Presentation phase: You open Copilot in PowerPoint with your analysis and memo and ask it to build a slide deck. It creates slides that match your company's template and pulls in the right data. Total time: 15 minutes. Building the presentation from scratch, even with AI help in a standalone chatbot, would take 45 minutes.

That's one workflow. Research in Perplexity, draft in Claude, analyze in ChatGPT, present in Copilot. Total: 45 minutes. Doing all of it in any single AI: easily two hours, with lower quality output.

The Learning Curve Is Real — But Short

I won't pretend there's no overhead. Learning multiple AI tools takes time. Each has its own interface, its own quirks, its own prompting sweet spots. You'll spend a week or two feeling slower as you figure out which tool to use for what.

But the curve is short. These tools are all conversational AI assistants at their core. If you know how to use one, you're 80% of the way to using any of them. The differences are in the details — and those details are what this book is here to teach you.

By the time you finish Part II of this book, you'll have a clear mental model: "This type of task goes to this AI." It'll become as natural as knowing that you open a browser for web stuff and a word processor for documents. You won't think about it. You'll just reach for the right tool.

Try This: Your First Multi-AI Test

Before you go further, try this. Take a question you actually care about — something related to your work, not a toy example. Something like "What are the best practices for remote team management in 2026?" or "How has the electric vehicle market changed in the last year?"

Ask the same question of three different AIs. Use whatever you have access to — ChatGPT, Claude, Gemini, Perplexity, it doesn't matter which three. Don't modify the question. Copy and paste the exact same prompt into each.

Now compare the results:

1. **Which response is most helpful?** Not longest — most helpful.
2. **Which one cites its sources?** Can you actually verify the claims?
3. **Which one is best organized?** Clear headers, logical flow, easy to scan?
4. **Which one tells you something you didn't know?**
5. **Which one would you trust enough to forward to your boss?**

Write down your answers. You've just started building your personal multi-AI intuition. The rest of this book is going to sharpen it.

A Day in the Life: Multi-AI in Practice

To make this concrete, let me walk you through a Tuesday for a marketing manager named Sarah. This isn't hypothetical — it's a composite of real workflows from people I've talked to who've internalized the multi-AI approach.

7:45 AM — Inbox triage. Sarah opens Outlook and sees 23 new emails. She uses Copilot to summarize the three longest threads, each with 15+ replies. In two minutes, she knows the state of three ongoing projects without reading a single full email. She dictates quick replies using Copilot's draft feature, tweaking tone from "casual" to "professional" on the one going to the VP.

8:30 AM — Competitive intel. Sarah's boss wants a briefing on a competitor's product launch from yesterday. She opens Perplexity and asks: "What did Acme Corp announce at their product event on March 28, 2026? Include pricing, key features, and analyst reactions." Perplexity returns a synthesis with twelve inline citations, including two analyst reports she hadn't seen. She clicks through the most relevant sources to verify the pricing details. Total time: eight minutes.

9:15 AM — Strategy memo. Sarah pastes her verified research notes into Claude and asks it to draft a competitive response memo for her leadership team. She includes her company's positioning and asks Claude to identify three areas where they have an advantage and two where they're vulnerable. Claude produces a 1,200-word memo that reads like Sarah wrote it on a good day. She edits for fifteen minutes — mostly adding internal context Claude couldn't know — and she's done.

11:00 AM — Data analysis. The Q1 campaign performance data arrived overnight. Sarah uploads the CSV to ChatGPT and asks: "Compare conversion rates across all channels, identify the three biggest quarter-over-quarter changes, and create a chart showing the trend for each channel." ChatGPT runs Python, produces three clean visualizations, and highlights that paid social dropped 22% while organic search climbed 15%. Sarah downloads the charts.

1:30 PM — Presentation. Sarah opens PowerPoint, pastes in her memo text and charts, and asks Copilot to "create a 10-slide executive briefing from this content, using our corporate template." Copilot generates the deck. It's not perfect — the data slides need rearranging and one chart title is wrong — but it's 80% there. She spends twenty minutes polishing instead of the ninety it would take from scratch.

3:00 PM — Creative brainstorm. The team needs campaign tagline options for the counter-positioning. Sarah opens ChatGPT and asks for twenty tagline ideas. ChatGPT delivers a range from safe to bold. She picks the three strongest, then takes them to Claude and asks: "Develop each of these taglines into a full campaign concept with messaging framework, target audience, and channel strategy." Claude turns three one-liners into three fleshed-out creative briefs.

4:30 PM — Quick research. A colleague in Slack asks whether their product's API pricing is competitive. Sarah @-mentions Claude in the channel, pastes in their pricing page URL and the competitor's, and asks for a comparison. Claude responds in the thread with a structured analysis the whole team can see.

Sarah used five different AI tools across her day. She didn't think about it any more than she thinks about whether to use email or Slack for a given message.

Each tool showed up where it was strongest, and the result was a day's worth of work that would have taken two days a year ago.

That's what the rest of this book is going to help you build.

The Bigger Picture

We're at an inflection point. The era of "one AI to rule them all" never materialized, and it's not going to. Instead, we're heading toward a world where using AI well means using multiple AIs well — knowing their strengths, compensating for their weaknesses, and chaining them together for outcomes no single tool can deliver alone.

This is good news. Competition between platforms means better features, lower prices, and more innovation. No single company controls the AI assistant market, and no single company's weaknesses become your permanent limitations.

The professionals who figure this out first will have a significant advantage. Not because they're smarter, but because they're more strategic about their tools.

Let's get you that advantage.

Chapter 2: How AI Assistants Actually Work

You don't need a PhD in machine learning to use AI assistants effectively. But understanding the basics of how they work — even at a high level — will make you dramatically better at using them. When you know *why* an AI gives you a 4,000-word answer when you wanted a tweet, or *why* it makes up a source that doesn't exist, or *why* it seems to forget what you told it earlier in the conversation, you can work around those behaviors instead of being frustrated by them.

This chapter gives you the mental model. No math. No jargon without explanation. Only the concepts that matter for getting better results.

Large Language Models: The Engine Under the Hood

Every major AI assistant — ChatGPT, Claude, Gemini, Copilot, even Perplexity — runs on a type of AI called a large language model, or LLM. Here's what that means in plain terms:

An LLM is a neural network — a software system loosely inspired by how brains process information — trained on enormous amounts of text. Trillions of words: books, websites, scientific papers, code repositories, forums, news articles, and much more.

During training, the model learns patterns. Not facts, exactly — patterns. It learns that after the words "the capital of France is," the word "Paris" is extremely likely to come next. It learns that code following a function definition should be indented. It learns that a business email usually ends with a sign-off. It learns thousands of these patterns, layered on top of each other at incredible depth.

When you type a prompt and hit enter, the model doesn't search a database. It doesn't look up the answer. It generates the response word by word (technically token by token, but we'll get to that), predicting the most likely next word given everything that came before.

This is both the magic and the limitation. It's magic because the predictions are so good the output reads like a knowledgeable human wrote it. It's a limitation because the model is doing sophisticated pattern matching, not reasoning from first principles or checking facts against a verified database.

Why this matters for you: When an AI confidently states something incorrect, it's not lying. It's predicting what a correct answer would look like based on patterns, and sometimes the patterns lead to the wrong place. That's why verification matters, and why some AIs are better at certain tasks — they were trained on different data or fine-tuned differently.

Tokens: The Currency of AI

AI models don't read words. They read tokens.

A token is a chunk of text — sometimes a whole word, sometimes part of a word, sometimes a punctuation mark. As a rough rule of thumb, one token is about three-quarters of a word in English. So 1,000 tokens is roughly 750 words.

Why should you care? Because tokens are the currency of AI in two ways:

Input tokens are what you send to the AI. Your prompt, any documents you paste in, the conversation history — all of it gets converted to tokens. Every AI has a limit on how many input tokens it can handle at once (more on this in the context window section below).

Output tokens are what the AI generates in response. Every word it writes back to you costs output tokens. On paid APIs, you pay per token. On consumer products, token limits are built into the pricing tiers.

Why this matters for you: When an AI cuts off its response mid-sentence, it usually hit its output token limit. When it can't "remember" something you told it earlier in a long conversation, the conversation may be approaching the input token limit and older content is being compressed or dropped. When a task seems expensive on an API, it's because it used a lot of tokens.

Different models have different costs per token, and those costs directly influence the pricing of the products built on them. That's one reason you see similar $20/month pricing across platforms — the underlying token economics are roughly similar.

Context Windows: The AI's Working Memory

The context window is one of the most important concepts for practical AI use. It's the total amount of text the AI can "see" at once — your prompt, the conversation history, any documents you've uploaded, and its own responses.

Think of it as the AI's working memory. Just as you can only hold so much in your head at once, an AI can only process so much text in a single interaction.

As of mid-2026, context windows vary significantly:

- **ChatGPT (GPT-5.5)**: 128K tokens (~96,000 words) on consumer tiers; larger on Enterprise
- **Claude (Sonnet 4.6/Opus 4.7)**: 1M tokens at standard pricing (~750,000 words)
- **Gemini (3.1 Pro)**: 1 million tokens on consumer plans (~750,000 words); Enterprise plans cap at 500K with stronger governance
- **Copilot**: Varies by integration, generally 128K tokens
- **Perplexity**: Varies, but typically smaller since it focuses on search-and-synthesize

Claude and Gemini both deliver 1M-token context windows on standard plans — large enough to hold multiple full-length novels or entire codebases in a single conversation. ChatGPT's 128K window handles almost any reasonable conversation or document.

But bigger isn't always better. Models with very large context windows sometimes show degraded performance on information in the "middle" of that window — a phenomenon researchers call "lost in the middle." The AI does great with what's at the beginning and end of its context, but can miss or underweight information buried in the middle of a long document.

Why this matters for you: If you're analyzing a long document, where you put the important parts matters. Put your question at the end, after the document. Put critical instructions at the beginning. If you're in a long conversation and the AI seems to have forgotten something, it's not being stubborn — it may have lost track. Start a new conversation with the key context explicitly restated.

Temperature and Creativity Settings

When an AI generates text, it doesn't just pick the single most likely next word every time. If it did, every response would be deterministic — the same prompt would always get the same answer, and the output would be bland and repetitive.

Instead, there's a setting called "temperature" that controls how much randomness (or "creativity") the model uses. At low temperature, the model mostly picks the most probable next token. At high temperature, it's more willing to pick less-obvious options, producing more varied, creative, and occasionally surprising output.

Most consumer AI products don't expose this setting directly. They pre-set temperature based on the task or offer options like "more creative" vs. "more precise." But understanding the concept explains why:

- The same prompt can give you different answers each time you ask it
- Asking for "creative" or "brainstorming" responses tends to produce more varied output
- Asking for factual or analytical responses tends to produce more consistent output
- Regenerating a response gives you a different answer, not just the same thing rephrased

Why this matters for you: If you need a specific, factual answer, tell the AI to be precise and stick to the facts. If you want creative options, ask for multiple alternatives. And if the first response isn't what you wanted, regenerating is a legitimate strategy — you might get something better on the second or third try.

Training Data and Knowledge Cutoffs

Every AI model was trained on data with a cutoff date. After that date, the model doesn't "know" what happened in the world unless it can access the internet in real time.

This is a crucial distinction between the model's built-in knowledge (from training) and real-time information (from web browsing or search). As of mid-2026:

- **ChatGPT**: GPT-5.5's training data extends through early 2026. ChatGPT can also browse the web for current information when you ask.
- **Claude**: Training data varies by model — January 2026 for Opus 4.7, August 2025 for Sonnet 4.6, July 2025 for Haiku 4.5. Claude has limited web search in its standard interface and can access documents you provide.
- **Gemini**: Regularly updated training data, plus deep integration with Google Search for current information.
- **Copilot**: Powered by OpenAI models (currently GPT-5.5) with Microsoft's own data integrations and Bing search.
- **Perplexity**: Always searches the web in real time — this is its entire point.

Why this matters for you: If you need current information, use a tool that can access the web (Perplexity, ChatGPT with browsing, or Gemini). If you're asking about timeless topics (how to structure an essay, explain a programming concept, analyze a philosophical argument), training data cutoffs are irrelevant and the model's built-in knowledge is usually enough.

RLHF: Why AIs Have Personalities

If you train a language model only on raw internet text and then ask it a question, you get something that sounds like the internet — a chaotic mix of helpful, unhelpful, toxic, and bizarre. Not great for a product.

So AI companies use a process called Reinforcement Learning from Human Feedback (RLHF) to shape the model's behavior. In short: human raters score the model's outputs, then the model is fine-tuned to produce more of what humans rated highly and less of what they rated poorly.

This is why different AI assistants have different "personalities":

- **ChatGPT** tends to be enthusiastic and eager to help, sometimes excessively so. It'll add flourishes and encouragement you didn't ask for.
- **Claude** tends to be more measured and thoughtful, sometimes overly cautious. It'll qualify its statements and flag uncertainties.
- **Gemini** tends to be concise and direct, sometimes to the point of being terse. It'll give you the answer without much elaboration.

- **Copilot** adapts its personality based on the integration — formal in Office, casual in chat, pragmatic in code.

These aren't superficial styling choices. They reflect deep differences in how each model was trained, what behaviors were rewarded, and what the company values. Anthropic (Claude's maker) is obsessed with safety and honesty, and it shows in Claude's cautious, thoughtful style. OpenAI optimized for broad user satisfaction, and it shows in ChatGPT's eager-to-please demeanor.

Why this matters for you: Different personalities suit different tasks. Claude's thoughtfulness is great for nuanced writing but can be annoying when you want a quick answer. ChatGPT's enthusiasm is great for brainstorming but can feel sycophantic when you want honest feedback. Match the personality to the task.

Multimodal Capabilities

Modern AI assistants aren't text-only. Most can now handle multiple types of input and output:

- **Vision**: Upload images and the AI can describe, analyze, or answer questions about them. All major models support this.
- **Image generation**: ChatGPT (via native GPT-5.5 image generation, building on the GPT-4o lineage), Gemini (via Imagen 4), and Copilot can generate images from text descriptions. Claude cannot generate images.
- **File handling**: Upload PDFs, Word docs, spreadsheets, and more for analysis. Support varies by platform.
- **Code execution**: ChatGPT's Advanced Data Analysis and Gemini can run code and return results. Claude can write code but typically doesn't execute it in-browser (though Claude Code does execute in a terminal environment).
- **Voice**: ChatGPT, Gemini, and Copilot offer voice conversation modes. Claude has added voice capabilities as well.
- **Video**: Gemini can analyze uploaded video. Other platforms are adding this capability.

Why this matters for you: The "best AI" for a task sometimes comes down to which input types it can handle. To analyze a chart from a screenshot, you need vision capabilities. To generate images, your options are more limited. Chapter 9 goes deep on creative capabilities.

How AI Assistants Handle Conversation

When you have a multi-turn conversation with an AI, something important is happening behind the scenes: the AI doesn't actually remember previous messages the way you do. Every time you send a new message, the *entire conversation history* is sent to the model as input. The model reads the whole thing from scratch and generates a response.

This has several practical implications:

1. **Conversations get "heavier" over time.** The more you chat, the more tokens are used for context, and the closer you get to the context window limit.

2. **Earlier messages have equal weight to later ones** (with the "lost in the middle" caveat mentioned above). The AI doesn't privilege recent messages over early ones — it considers the whole context.

3. **Starting a new conversation is a clean slate.** The AI has zero memory of previous conversations (unless the platform has a memory feature, which some do).

4. **System prompts matter.** Most platforms let you set instructions that persist across a conversation (like ChatGPT's Custom Instructions or Claude's Project Instructions). These shape every response in that conversation.

Why this matters for you: For complex projects, don't try to do everything in one marathon conversation. Break work into focused sessions. When starting a new conversation, provide context upfront — don't assume the AI remembers what you discussed last time.

Try This: See the Differences in Action

Open two different AI assistants side by side. Give each one this exact prompt:

> "Explain quantum computing to a smart 12-year-old in exactly 100 words."

Compare the results: - Did both hit the word count? (They probably didn't — word counting is surprisingly hard for LLMs.) - Which explanation is clearer? - Which one uses better analogies? - Which one sounds more like a human teacher?

Now try: "Write a haiku about debugging code."

Compare the creativity, the humor, the adherence to the 5-7-5 syllable structure. You'll see the personality differences immediately.

These aren't just fun exercises. They build your intuition for what each AI does well. And that intuition is the foundation of everything that follows.

The Key Takeaway

AI assistants are sophisticated pattern-matching machines with different training data, different optimizations, and different personalities. They don't "know" things the way you do — they predict likely text. Understanding this doesn't diminish their usefulness. It makes you better at using them.

Once you understand that a model is predicting tokens, you understand why it sometimes makes things up. Once you understand context windows, you know why long conversations go sideways. Once you understand RLHF, you know why Claude sounds different from ChatGPT. Once you understand temperature, you know why regenerating a response might give you something better.

This is the foundation. Now let's meet the players.

Chapter 3: The Major Players

Time for introductions. This chapter profiles every AI assistant you need to know about in 2026 — not just what the company says their product does, but what it actually does well, where it falls short, and who it's really for.

I'll be honest in these profiles. Every platform has marketing that makes it sound like the answer to everything. None of them are. Let's talk about what's real.

ChatGPT (OpenAI)

The pitch: The original mainstream AI assistant, now a mature platform that handles text, images, code, web browsing, file analysis, voice conversation, and custom GPTs.

The model: GPT-5.5 is the flagship as of mid-2026 (GPT-5.5 Thinking for the deepest reasoning), with GPT-5.5 mini for lighter tasks. The earlier o-series of reasoning models has been absorbed into the GPT-5.x Thinking line.

What it actually does best: - **Broad generalist work.** ChatGPT is the Swiss Army knife. For any given task, it's rarely the worst option and often a good-enough option. If you could only pick one AI, ChatGPT would be the safest bet. - **Data analysis.** Advanced Data Analysis (formerly Code Interpreter) lets you upload files, run Python, and get visualizations — all inside the chat interface. For CSV analysis, charting, and quick data exploration, it's still the best-in-class experience. - **Image generation.** ChatGPT's native image generation (built on the GPT-4o lineage and carried forward into GPT-5.x) is remarkably capable — photorealistic images, text rendering, style matching. It surpassed standalone DALL-E and has become the benchmark for AI image generation in a chatbot interface. - **Plugins and GPTs.** The GPT Store offers thousands of custom assistants, and building your own GPTs is straightforward. The ecosystem is the largest. - **Voice conversation.** ChatGPT's Advanced Voice Mode is fluid and natural, supporting real-time conversation with emotional nuance.

Where it falls short: - **Writing quality for long-form content.** ChatGPT tends toward a recognizable "AI voice" — enthusiastic, slightly generic, with a fondness for bullet points and words like "delve" and "tapestry." It's improved, but it still requires more editing than Claude for polished prose. - **Sycophancy.**

ChatGPT has a well-documented tendency to agree with you, praise your ideas, and tell you what you want to hear. That's actively harmful when you need honest feedback. - **Citations.** When browsing the web, ChatGPT provides sources, but they're less consistently accurate than Perplexity's. - **Following complex instructions.** For multi-step, heavily constrained prompts, ChatGPT sometimes drops requirements or partially follows them.

Pricing: Free tier available (GPT-5.5 mini with limits). ChatGPT Plus is $20/month. Team and Enterprise tiers available.

Best for: Generalists, data analysts, people who want one tool that does most things reasonably well, image generation.

Claude (Anthropic)

The pitch: An AI assistant built by a safety-focused research lab, known for thoughtful writing, large context windows, careful reasoning, and strong coding capabilities.

The model: Claude Opus 4.7 (released April 2026) is the top-tier model, with Sonnet 4.6 as the workhorse and Haiku 4.5 for fast, lightweight tasks. Both Sonnet 4.6 and Opus 4.7 ship with a 1M-token context window at standard pricing.

What it actually does best: - **Long-form writing.** This is Claude's signature strength. For memos, reports, essays, articles, documentation, and any writing that needs to sound like a human wrote it, Claude produces output that requires the least editing of any major AI. The prose is more natural, the structure more thoughtful, the tone more adaptable. - **Careful reasoning and analysis.** Claude is less likely to make confident-sounding errors. It hedges when it should hedge, qualifies when it should qualify, and admits uncertainty when it's uncertain. For tasks where accuracy matters more than speed, that's valuable. - **Large document analysis.** Claude's 1M-token context window lets you upload substantial documents — entire contracts, codebases, research papers — and work with them coherently. - **Coding.** Claude Code, a terminal-based coding assistant, has become a serious tool for software development. For writing new code, refactoring, and understanding complex codebases, Claude is competitive with or ahead of the field. - **Following complex instructions.** Claude is notably good at following detailed, multi-step prompts faithfully. Give it a complex brief with many requirements and it's more likely to hit all of them.

Where it falls short: - **No native image generation.** Claude cannot create images. If you need image generation, you need a different tool. - **Web access.** Claude has limited web search capabilities, and it isn't its primary strength. You'll get the best results by providing documents directly or working from Claude's training data. - **Data visualization.** Claude can write code that generates charts, but it doesn't execute that code in-browser the way ChatGPT does. You need to run it yourself (or use Claude Code in a development environment). - **Overcaution.** Claude sometimes refuses tasks or adds excessive caveats. A request to write a villain's dialogue might get a disclaimer about portraying negative behavior. This has improved significantly but remains a factor. - **Shorter responses by default.** Claude can be concise to a fault, requiring you to explicitly ask for longer, more detailed output.

Pricing: Free tier available (Sonnet with limits). Claude Pro is $20/month. Team and Enterprise tiers available.

Best for: Writers, analysts, developers (especially via Claude Code), anyone working with long documents, anyone who values accuracy over speed.

Gemini (Google)

The pitch: Google's AI assistant, deeply integrated with Google's ecosystem and powered by models with enormous context windows.

The model: Gemini 3.1 Pro is the flagship (Gemini 3 Pro for the broader tier), with Gemini 3 Flash and Gemini 3.1 Flash-Lite offering faster, lighter alternatives.

What it actually does best: - **Google ecosystem integration.** If you live in Google Workspace — Gmail, Docs, Sheets, Slides, Calendar, Drive — Gemini works with all of it. Summarize an email thread, draft a response, analyze a spreadsheet, create slides from a document. No copying and pasting between apps. - **Massive context window.** Gemini 3.1 Pro supports up to 1 million tokens at standard pricing — large enough to hold multiple full-length novels. You can upload entire codebases, multiple long documents, even hours of video for analysis. Enterprise plans cap at 500K tokens with stronger governance features. - **Multimodal understanding.** Gemini handles text, images, audio, and video as native input types. Its video analysis is ahead of the competition. -

Google Search integration. When Gemini searches the web, it uses Google Search — the best search engine in the world. For current-events questions, that's a significant advantage. - **Speed.** Gemini Flash models are among the fastest available, providing near-instant responses for quick queries.

Where it falls short: - **Writing quality.** Gemini's output tends to be more concise and less polished than Claude's or even ChatGPT's. For long-form writing, it often produces shorter output than you want and requires more rounds of prompting to reach the desired depth. - **Instruction following.** For complex, multi-constraint prompts, Gemini sometimes simplifies or drops requirements. It gets the gist but may miss the details. - **Creative writing.** For fiction, creative nonfiction, or anything requiring distinctive voice and style, Gemini trails Claude and ChatGPT. - **Inconsistency.** In my testing, Gemini's output quality varies more run-to-run than other models. The same prompt can produce a great response one time and a mediocre one the next.

Pricing: Free tier (Gemini 2.5 Flash). Google AI Plus at $7.99/month (launched January 2026), Google AI Pro at $19.99/month (Gemini 3 Pro plus 1,000 AI credits), and Google AI Ultra at $249.99/month (Gemini 3.1 Pro, Deep Think, Veo 3.1, 25,000 credits).

Best for: Google Workspace users, people who need to process very large or multimodal inputs, anyone who values ecosystem integration over standalone quality.

Copilot (Microsoft)

The pitch: Microsoft's AI assistant, embedded across Windows, Office 365, Edge, and GitHub. Goes where you already work.

The model: Powered by OpenAI's GPT-5.x family (GPT-5.5 by default; GPT-5.4 Think Deeper or GPT-5.5 Thinking when extended reasoning is invoked), wrapped in Microsoft's Smart/Quick Response/Think Deeper mode picker and ecosystem integrations.

What it actually does best: - **Office 365 integration.** Copilot in Word can draft, rewrite, and summarize documents. Copilot in Excel can analyze data, create charts, and write formulas. Copilot in PowerPoint can generate presentations from outlines or documents. Copilot in Outlook can draft emails and summarize threads. Copilot in Teams can summarize meetings, identify action items, and answer questions about what was discussed. - **GitHub Copilot for code.** GitHub Copilot is arguably the most widely used AI coding tool. Its inline code suggestions, chat-in-IDE experience, and deep integration with VS Code and JetBrains make it the default choice for many developers. - **Windows integration.** Copilot in Windows provides system-level AI access: ask questions, change settings, open apps, summarize content on screen. - **Enterprise readiness.** Microsoft 365 Copilot has enterprise-grade security, compliance, and admin controls that many organizations require.

Where it falls short: - **Standalone chat quality.** Copilot's standalone chat experience (in Edge or Bing) is less polished than ChatGPT, Claude, or Gemini. It's best when embedded in other Microsoft products. - **Model freshness.** Copilot often uses older or less capable OpenAI models than ChatGPT itself. The "same AI" sometimes feels like a watered-down version. - **Creative tasks.** Copilot isn't where you go for creative writing, brainstorming, or nuanced analysis. It's built for productivity, not creativity. - **Cost for businesses.** Microsoft 365 Copilot Enterprise costs $30/user/month and the new Microsoft 365 E7 "Frontier Suite" (May 2026) bundles it with Agent 365 governance for $99/user/month. The smaller-org Copilot Business tier runs $18–21/user/month. On top of existing Microsoft 365 licensing, that still adds up fast for large organizations.

Pricing: Copilot Chat (free, basic features). Copilot Pro is $20/month. Microsoft 365 Copilot Business is $18–21/user/month; Microsoft 365 Copilot Enterprise is $30/user/month; the E7 Frontier Suite (Copilot + Agent 365 + Entra Suite + E5) is $99/user/month. Agent 365 standalone is $15/user/month. GitHub Copilot is $10/month (Pro), $39/month (Pro+), $19/user/month (Business), or $39/user/month (Enterprise) — with usage-based billing via GitHub AI Credits beginning June 1, 2026.

Best for: Microsoft Office users, developers (via GitHub Copilot), enterprise environments, anyone who wants AI embedded in their existing productivity tools.

Perplexity

The pitch: An AI-powered answer engine that searches the web in real time and provides cited, synthesized answers.

The model: Perplexity uses multiple underlying models (including its own fine-tuned models and third-party models) and combines them with real-time web search.

What it actually does best: - **Research with citations.** This is Perplexity's entire reason for existing, and it's the best at it. Every claim comes with an inline citation you can click to verify. For research, fact-finding, and staying current, nothing else comes close. - **Current information.** While other AIs have training data cutoffs, Perplexity searches the web for every query. For "what happened today" or "what's the latest on X," Perplexity delivers genuinely current answers. - **Academic research.** Perplexity's academic focus mode searches scholarly databases and provides citations in proper formats. For literature reviews and academic research, that's useful. - **Follow-up questions.** Perplexity excels at iterative research — you ask a question, get an answer, and ask follow-up questions that build on the previous context. It's like having a research assistant who remembers what you've already found. - **Transparency.** You can always see where the information came from. That's a fundamentally different trust model from AIs that generate text from training data without attribution.

Where it falls short: - **Not a general-purpose assistant.** Perplexity isn't designed for writing, coding, data analysis, or creative work. It's a research tool. Using it to write a memo is like using a search engine to write a memo — technically possible but not what it's built for. - **Limited output depth.** Perplexity's answers are thorough but concise. It synthesizes and summarizes; it doesn't produce long-form content. - **Limited file handling.** Perplexity Pro supports file uploads, but document analysis isn't Perplexity's core strength. It's a research and search tool first; for deep document analysis, Claude or ChatGPT serve you better. - **No code execution.** No data analysis, no chart generation, no running Python.

Pricing: Free tier available (limited searches). Perplexity Pro is $20/month.

Best for: Researchers, journalists, anyone who needs current, cited information, anyone tired of AI hallucinations.

The Emerging Players

Beyond the big five, several other AI assistants are worth watching:

Grok (xAI): Elon Musk's AI, integrated with X (formerly Twitter). It has real-time access to posts on X and takes a more irreverent, unfiltered tone. Useful for tracking social media discourse, less proven for professional tasks.

Meta AI (Meta): Powered by Meta's Llama models, integrated into WhatsApp, Instagram, and Facebook. Its primary advantage is reaching billions of people who already use Meta's platforms. The standalone capability trails the leaders, but the reach is enormous.

Mistral (Mistral AI): A French AI company producing competitive open-weight models. Le Chat, their consumer product, is fast and capable. Worth watching as a viable European alternative.

DeepSeek: A Chinese AI company that has produced models competitive with Western leaders at substantially lower cost. The current flagship DeepSeek-V4 (April 2026) ships in two MIT-licensed open-weight variants — V4 Pro (1.6T total/49B active) and V4 Flash (284B/13B), both with 1M-token context — at roughly 1/7 the per-token cost of Claude Opus 4.7 on coding workloads. The geopolitical implications of using a China-jurisdiction hosted API are complex; the open weights also enable self-hosting that sidesteps the jurisdiction question.

OpenClaw: An open-source agentic-AI framework that runs locally and integrates with messaging apps (Signal, Telegram, Discord, WhatsApp). Created by Peter Steinberger in late 2025, it crossed 310,000 GitHub stars by spring 2026 and is now stewarded by a non-profit foundation after Steinberger joined OpenAI in February 2026. Notable for its skills system, local-first architecture, and the "Agents of Chaos" research that documented eleven failure modes in agentic AI.

Local/Open Source: Models like Llama, Mistral, and others can run locally on your own hardware using tools like Ollama. That gives you complete privacy but requires technical setup and powerful hardware for good performance.

How They Stack Up

Here's the honest summary:

Strength	Leader	Runner-Up
Overall generalist	ChatGPT	Claude
Long-form writing	Claude	ChatGPT

Strength	Leader	Runner-Up
Research with citations	Perplexity	Gemini
Data analysis	ChatGPT	Gemini
Image generation	ChatGPT	Gemini
Coding (IDE)	GitHub Copilot	Claude Code
Coding (chat)	Claude	ChatGPT
Office integration	Copilot	Gemini
Large context	Gemini	Claude
Video analysis	Gemini	ChatGPT
Privacy/safety	Claude	ChatGPT
Speed	Gemini Flash	Claude Haiku

This table is a simplification. The chapters that follow will go deep on each use case with nuance and caveats. But if you need a quick reference for "which one should I try first," this is your starting point.

Try This: Meet Everyone

If you haven't already, create a free account on each of the five major platforms: - chatgpt.com (ChatGPT) - claude.ai (Claude) - gemini.google.com (Gemini) - copilot.microsoft.com (Copilot) - perplexity.ai (Perplexity)

All five offer free tiers. You won't get the full power of any of them without paying, but you'll get enough to start developing instincts for what each one feels like.

Ask each one: "What are you best at, and what are you worst at?" The answers are revealing — not just for what they say, but for how they say it. ChatGPT will give you an enthusiastic, balanced response. Claude will give you a thoughtful, qualified one. Gemini will be brief. Perplexity will search for articles about itself. Copilot will tell you about Microsoft products.

Welcome to the landscape. Now let's figure out how to navigate it.

Chapter 4: Choosing the Right AI for the Task

This is the chapter you'll come back to — the one you'll dog-ear, bookmark, or screenshot. Because the most valuable skill in the multi-AI landscape isn't writing better prompts. It's knowing which AI to open in the first place.

The framework that follows isn't drawn from marketing materials or benchmark scores. It comes from hundreds of hours of testing real tasks. It's opinionated, specific, and will save you a lot of time.

The Decision Framework

Before you reach for any AI, ask yourself three questions:

1. **What type of task is this?** (Writing, research, analysis, coding, creative, communication)
2. **What matters most for this task?** (Accuracy, speed, polish, integration, creativity)
3. **Where does the output need to end up?** (Document, email, code, presentation, social post)

The combination of those three answers points you to the right tool almost every time.

Let me walk you through each.

By Task Type

"I need to write something."

Reach for: Claude.

Claude produces the most natural, well-structured, publication-ready prose of any AI assistant. Whether it's a business memo, a blog post, a report, or a personal essay, Claude's output reads like a skilled human wrote it. You'll spend less time editing, and your edits will be refinements rather than rewrites.

Exceptions: - If the writing ends up in a Google Doc and you're already in Workspace, Gemini is faster because it skips the copy-paste step. - If the writing is a short social media post or ad copy, ChatGPT is equally good and often more energetic. - If the writing needs current facts and citations, research in Perplexity first, then bring the findings to Claude for drafting.

"I need to find something out."

Reach for: Perplexity.

For any question where you need current, accurate information with sources you can verify, Perplexity is the clear winner. It searches the web, synthesizes results, and provides inline citations for every claim. This isn't a close call.

Exceptions: - If the question is timeless (how does photosynthesis work, what is supply-chain management), any AI's training data suffices and Perplexity is overkill. - If you need a quick fact and you're already mid-conversation with another AI, just ask it rather than context-switching. - If your research is deep analysis of a document you already have (not a web search), Claude is better. Perplexity Pro supports file uploads, but document analysis isn't its core strength.

"I need to analyze data."

Reach for: ChatGPT.

ChatGPT's Advanced Data Analysis lets you upload CSVs, Excel files, and other formats, runs Python on them, and generates charts and visualizations — all inside the chat window. The experience is polished: upload a file, describe what you want to know, and get answers with downloadable visualizations.

Exceptions: - If the data lives in a Google Sheet, Gemini can work with it directly — no export needed. - If the data lives in Excel and you want analysis inside the spreadsheet, Copilot in Excel is the tool. - If you need a complex, reproducible data pipeline rather than a quick analysis, write the code in Claude Code or with GitHub Copilot.

"I need to write or debug code."

This depends on context. There's no single winner for all coding tasks.

- **Inline code completion in your IDE**: GitHub Copilot. The most seamless experience for writing code as you type.
- **Building or refactoring a feature via conversation**: Claude (via claude.ai or Claude Code). Claude's code is consistently well-structured, well-commented, and architecturally sound.
- **Quick scripts and one-off code tasks**: ChatGPT. Upload a file, describe what you need, and ChatGPT will write and often execute the code.
- **Code in Google's ecosystem**: Gemini Code Assist, especially in Android Studio or Google Cloud.

"I need to create images or visual content."

Reach for: ChatGPT.

ChatGPT's native image generation (the GPT-4o capability carried forward into GPT-5.x) produces high-quality images with strong text rendering, style consistency, and creative range. As of mid-2026, it's the most capable image generator embedded in a general-purpose AI assistant.

Exceptions: - For specific artistic styles or maximum customization, standalone tools like Midjourney or Stable Diffusion may serve you better. - Gemini's Imagen is competitive and improving rapidly. - For images inside a Google Slides presentation, Gemini is more convenient.

"I need to do something in my productivity suite."

Reach for: whatever's built into your suite.

- Microsoft Office 365 user? Copilot.
- Google Workspace user? Gemini.

Not because Copilot and Gemini are better models, but because integration saves enormous time. Drafting an email in Outlook with Copilot takes ten seconds. Copying a ChatGPT draft into Outlook and formatting it takes two minutes. For embedded tasks, integration trumps raw model quality.

By What Matters Most

Sometimes the task type doesn't tell the whole story. Here's how to decide when you need a specific quality:

"Accuracy is paramount."

Reach for: Perplexity for factual claims, Claude for reasoning.

If you're writing something that will be publicly attributed to you — a report, an executive presentation, an article — accuracy matters more than speed. Perplexity gives you cited facts. Claude gives you careful reasoning that's less likely to contain confident errors.

Avoid: ChatGPT for factual claims without verification. Its eagerness to give definitive answers sometimes outpaces its accuracy.

"Speed is paramount."

Reach for: Gemini Flash or Claude Haiku.

When you just need a quick answer — a synonym, a formula, a fast explanation — the fastest model wins. Gemini Flash and Claude Haiku both respond in under a second.

If you're already in a conversation with any AI, just ask. Don't context-switch for speed-priority tasks.

"Polish is paramount."

Reach for: Claude for text, ChatGPT for visuals.

"Polish" means output that's close to final quality with minimal editing. For text, Claude consistently produces the most polished output. For images and visual content, ChatGPT leads.

"I need creative options."

Reach for: ChatGPT for brainstorming, Claude for depth.

ChatGPT excels at generating lots of ideas fast. Ask for ten taglines, twenty names, five approaches. Claude excels at developing any one idea in depth. The optimal creative workflow is often: brainstorm in ChatGPT, develop the best idea in Claude.

"I need honesty, not encouragement."

Reach for: Claude.

If you want real feedback on your writing, business plan, or strategy, Claude is the least likely to just tell you it's great. Claude identifies weaknesses, suggests improvements, and pushes back on flawed reasoning. ChatGPT tells you everything is wonderful and you're brilliant. That feels nice but isn't useful.

The Quick-Reference Decision Matrix

Here's the distilled version. Print this out or save it on your phone:

I need to...	First choice	Why
Write a memo or report	Claude	Best prose, least editing
Research a topic	Perplexity	Cited, current, verified
Analyze a spreadsheet	ChatGPT	Best data analysis UX
Write code (IDE)	GitHub Copilot	Seamless inline completion
Write code (conversation)	Claude	Best code quality
Generate images	ChatGPT	Best image generation
Process a long document	Claude	1M-token context window
Process video	Gemini	Best video analysis
Draft an Office document	Copilot	Native integration
Draft a Google Doc	Gemini	Native integration
Brainstorm ideas	ChatGPT	High-volume creativity
Get honest feedback	Claude	Least sycophantic
Quick factual question	Whichever's open	Not worth switching
Current events	Perplexity	Real-time search
Summarize a meeting	Copilot (Teams)	Native recording access

When the Framework Breaks Down

This framework covers 80–90% of situations. Here's when it doesn't apply:

When you're already mid-conversation. If you've built up significant context in a ChatGPT conversation and need to write a paragraph, don't switch to Claude just because Claude writes better prose. The context is worth more than the marginal quality bump. Switch tools at natural breakpoints, not mid-stream.

When company policy dictates. Many organizations mandate specific AI tools for security, compliance, or licensing reasons. Follow your organization's policy, even if a different tool would theoretically suit the task better.

When you need consistency. If you're producing a series of related documents, using the same AI for all of them keeps tone and style consistent. Switching mid-project can create jarring inconsistencies.

When the stakes are low. If you're drafting a grocery list or a message to a friend, don't overthink it. Use whatever's closest. The framework is for work that matters.

Building Your Instinct

You might be reading this matrix and thinking, "I'll never remember all of this." You will. It takes about two weeks of conscious practice before it becomes instinct.

Here's how to speed it up:

1. **For one week, before every AI interaction, pause and ask: "Is this the right tool for this task?"** Check the matrix. Pick accordingly. Yes, this slows you down. That's temporary.
2. **Keep a simple log.** Nothing fancy. Just: Task | Tool Used | Result (good/fair/poor). After a week, patterns emerge.
3. **When a result is poor, try the same task in a different AI.** Compare. This is how you calibrate your instincts.
4. **After two weeks, stop checking the matrix.** You'll already know which tool to reach for. The matrix has become instinct.

Try This: Run the Framework

Take three real tasks from your actual workday — not hypotheticals. Before each one, consult the matrix and pick the recommended tool. Do the task. Then assess honestly: was the result better than what you'd have gotten from your default AI?

If you default to ChatGPT for everything, try Claude for your next writing task and Perplexity for your next research task. Just those two changes will likely show a noticeable jump in output quality.

The goal isn't to make your life more complicated. It's to make your output better with the same effort. The right tool for the right task isn't more work — it's less, because you spend less time editing, verifying, and redoing.

Decision Scenarios: Real Situations, Specific Recommendations

The framework above covers the general principles. But real life is messier than a matrix. Here are scenarios I hit regularly, with my recommended approach.

Scenario: "I need to prepare for a job interview at a company I don't know well." Start in Perplexity: "What are the major challenges facing [Company] in 2026? Include recent news, earnings data, and analyst commentary." Perplexity gives you cited, current intelligence you can verify. Then move to Claude: "Based on these findings, what are the five most impressive questions I could ask in an interview for a [Role] position at this company?" Claude crafts thoughtful, specific questions that signal real research. Skip ChatGPT here — it's more likely to give you generic interview advice than company-specific insight.

Scenario: "I have a 45-page PDF contract and need to understand what I'm signing." This is Claude, no question. Upload the PDF (Claude's context window handles it easily) and ask: "Identify the five most important clauses in this contract, any unusual terms that deviate from standard agreements, and anything I should negotiate before signing. Explain each in plain language." Claude will be thorough, careful, and honest about what's concerning. ChatGPT will give you a reasonable summary, but Claude is less likely to gloss over something that matters.

Scenario: "I need to turn raw survey data into a board-ready report." A three-tool workflow. Upload the raw data to ChatGPT and ask for statistical analysis, key findings, and visualizations. Take those findings to Claude for the narrative report — the "what it means" section that boards actually read. Then open Copilot in PowerPoint to assemble the final deck using your company template. Each tool handles the phase it's best at.

Scenario: "My team is debating two strategic directions and we need a structured analysis." Claude. Ask it to build a decision matrix with weighted criteria, evaluate both options against each, surface the key assumptions behind each, and recommend which assumptions to test before committing. Claude's willingness to say "this depends on X, which you haven't determined yet" is exactly what strategic decisions need. ChatGPT would give you an answer; Claude gives you a framework for finding the answer.

Scenario: "I need to write a cold outreach email that actually gets responses." Start with ChatGPT for volume: "Give me 10 different angles for a cold email to [persona] about [product]." Pick the angle that resonates. Then take it to Claude: "Write a cold email using this angle. Keep it under 150 words. Tone: direct, respectful, no hype. The ask is a 15-minute call, not a sale." Claude produces something concise and human-sounding. ChatGPT's version will run longer and more sales-flavored than you want.

Scenario: "I need to explain a technical concept to a non-technical stakeholder." Claude handles this translation work exceptionally well. Upload or paste the technical content and say: "Rewrite this for a VP of Marketing with no technical background. Use analogies. Keep it under 500 words. The goal is that they grasp the business impact, not the technical details." Claude consistently nails the balance between accuracy and accessibility.

Scenario: "I'm writing a blog post and need to make sure my facts are right." Draft wherever you prefer (Claude for quality, ChatGPT for speed). Then take specific factual claims to Perplexity: "Verify each of these claims and provide sources: [paste claims]." Perplexity checks each one against current sources and flags anything it can't confirm. Faster and more reliable than asking your drafting AI to fact-check its own work.

The Meta-Skill

Choosing the right AI is itself a skill. Like any skill, it starts out conscious and effortful and becomes automatic with practice. The knowledge workers who master this in 2026 will have a real edge over those who stick with one tool out of habit or loyalty.

You're not being disloyal to ChatGPT by using Claude for writing. You're not cheating on Claude by using Perplexity for research. You're being strategic. In a landscape where everyone has access to the same AI tools, strategy is what separates the people who use AI well from the people who just use AI.

The next several chapters go deep on specific use cases. Each refines and expands the framework for its domain. Consider this chapter the map. The next ones are the street-level guides.

Part II: Task-Based AI Selection

"To the man who only has a hammer, everything he encounters begins to look like a nail."

— Abraham Maslow

Chapter 5: Writing and Editing

Writing is the most common task people bring to AI assistants, and it's where platform differences show up most clearly. Within ten minutes of testing, you can feel the gap between an AI that produces generic, over-enthusiastic prose and one that writes like a thoughtful human. This chapter goes deep on those differences and tells you exactly which tool to reach for depending on what you're writing.

The Writing Quality Spectrum

The ranking as of early 2026, plainly:

1. **Claude** — the best overall writer among AI assistants
2. **ChatGPT** — a solid second, better for specific formats
3. **Gemini** — capable but tends toward brevity and blandness
4. **Copilot** — good within Office, weaker standalone
5. **Perplexity** — not a writing tool (don't use it for this)

That's the headline. What "better" means in practice varies by the type of writing.

Long-Form Writing: Reports, Memos, Articles

This is where Claude's advantage is most pronounced. Ask Claude for a 2,000-word strategy memo, a detailed report, or a long-form article, and the output has qualities that set it apart:

Natural prose rhythm. Claude varies sentence length and structure in ways that feel human. It avoids the "short sentence. Long sentence with many clauses, commas, and qualifying phrases. Short sentence again." pattern ChatGPT often produces.

Thoughtful structure. Claude organizes ideas in a logical flow that doesn't always lean on bullet points and headers. It writes sustained paragraphs that develop an argument — essential for anything that will be read as continuous prose.

Tone adaptability. Tell Claude to write formally and it does. Tell it to write conversationally and it shifts naturally. ChatGPT can do this too, but its "conversational" mode often comes out as "corporate trying to sound casual." Claude's feels more genuinely relaxed.

Restraint. Claude doesn't overuse superlatives, doesn't pile on enthusiasm, and doesn't pad output with filler. ChatGPT will call something "truly remarkable" and "absolutely fascinating" when "notable" and "interesting" would do. Claude uses the right-sized word.

Try This: The Memo Test

Open both Claude and ChatGPT. Give each this exact prompt:

> "Write a 1,500-word internal memo to my team explaining why we're switching from Slack to Microsoft Teams. The reasons are: cost savings ($4 per user per month), better integration with our existing Office 365 tools, and the new AI features in Teams. The tone should be honest and empathetic — the team likes Slack and won't be happy about this. Address their likely concerns."

Read both outputs. Pay attention to: - Does it sound like a real memo from a real manager, or like an AI wrote it? - Does it actually address the team's likely frustration, or hand-wave past it? - Is the tone empathetic without being patronizing? - Would you send it as-is, or does it need significant editing?

In my testing, Claude's version needs light editing. ChatGPT's needs moderate restructuring and a tone adjustment to sound less like a press release.

Short-Form Writing: Emails, Social Posts, Quick Messages

For short-form content, the gap between Claude and ChatGPT narrows considerably. In a three-paragraph email or a tweet, prose nuance matters less. Speed and format-awareness matter more.

ChatGPT has an edge for: - Marketing copy and ad text (it's more energetic and punchy) - Social media posts (it understands platform conventions well) - Cold outreach emails (it's better at the persuasive, upbeat tone these require) - Brainstorming taglines, subject lines, and headlines

Claude has an edge for: - Sensitive communications (bad news, apologies, delicate situations) - Professional correspondence where tone precision matters -

Follow-up emails that need to reference complex context - Any email longer than a few paragraphs

Gemini works well for: - Quick email drafts within Gmail (integration advantage) - Summarizing email threads and drafting replies - Any writing that needs to stay within the Google ecosystem

Editing and Rewriting

Here's an underused case: AI as editor for writing you've already done — not as ghostwriter. It's one of the highest-value uses of AI, and the platforms differ in meaningful ways.

Copy Editing

For catching grammar, spelling, punctuation, and clarity issues in existing text:

Claude is the best editor. Give it your text and say "edit this for clarity, grammar, and flow, but preserve my voice." Claude makes surgical improvements without rewriting everything. It respects the author's style while fixing real issues.

ChatGPT tends to over-edit. It has a strong instinct to "improve" text by making it sound more like ChatGPT. Give it a casual email and you might get back something that reads like a TED talk. You can mitigate this with explicit instructions ("make minimal changes, only fix errors"), but it takes more prompt engineering.

Gemini is decent at identifying issues but sometimes introduces new errors while fixing others. Check its edits carefully.

Rewriting for Tone

"Make this more professional" or "make this more casual" — every AI handles this, but with different defaults:

- **Claude** shifts tone subtly and naturally. The rewrite feels like the same person writing for a different audience.
- **ChatGPT** shifts tone more dramatically. The rewrite can feel like a different person entirely.

- **Gemini** handles tone shifts well inside Google Docs, where you can highlight text and request a rewrite in context.

Restructuring

For taking a messy draft and reorganizing it into a coherent structure:

Claude excels here. Give it a rambling first draft and ask for a restructure without losing content. It identifies the core arguments, finds the logical order, and reorganizes while keeping your points intact.

ChatGPT is good at this too, but it's more likely to drop or summarize content during restructuring. Always compare the restructured version against the original to make sure nothing was lost.

Style and Voice Consistency

One of the trickier challenges in AI-assisted writing is keeping a consistent voice, especially across multiple documents or with multiple contributors.

Using Style References

The most effective technique is giving the AI a sample of the desired style. This works across all platforms, but quality varies:

Claude is the best at absorbing and reproducing a specific style. Hand it 500 words of sample writing and say "match this style," and the output reads like the same author.

ChatGPT can match style but tends to exaggerate distinctive features. If your style is slightly informal, ChatGPT goes aggressively casual. If your style is slightly formal, ChatGPT goes full academic.

Gemini approximates style but misses nuance. It gets the broad strokes right but loses the subtle rhythms.

Try This: The Voice Match

Find a piece of writing you've done that you're proud of — an email, a blog post, a report. Give it to both Claude and ChatGPT with this prompt:

> "Here's a sample of my writing style. Study it carefully — the tone, vocabulary, sentence structure, and personality. Then write a new piece in the same style about [new topic]. Match my voice as closely as possible."

Compare the two results against your original. Which one sounds more like you?

Specialized Writing Tasks

Academic and Technical Writing

Claude leads for academic writing. It knows the conventions of scholarly prose, handles citations properly (always verify), and produces output that reads like it belongs in a journal or thesis.

ChatGPT is good for technical documentation and API docs. Its structure suits step-by-step technical content.

Gemini can help with academic research drafts thanks to its Google Scholar integration, but the writing quality itself sits below Claude and ChatGPT.

Creative Writing: Fiction and Poetry

Creative writing is interesting because the "best" AI depends on what you want:

Claude writes the most literary fiction. Its prose has more subtlety, its dialogue feels more natural, its characters develop with more nuance. For literary fiction or creative nonfiction, Claude is the clear choice.

ChatGPT is better for genre fiction — thriller plots, fantasy world-building, romance dialogue. It's more willing to be dramatic and less worried about subtlety.

Gemini is the weakest for creative writing. Its output tends toward safe and generic.

Business Writing

For business-specific formats — proposals, business plans, executive summaries, investor decks:

Claude produces the most credible, professional output. Its business writing reads like an experienced consultant wrote it, not an AI.

ChatGPT is better for persuasive business writing — pitch decks, marketing proposals, grant applications. Its enthusiasm works in your favor here.

Copilot has the edge when the writing lives inside Office documents, especially when it can pull from company data in SharePoint or other Microsoft 365 sources.

The Multi-AI Writing Workflow

The workflow I use for important writing projects, which consistently produces the best results:

1. **Research in Perplexity.** Gather facts, data, and sources. Save the citations.
2. **Outline in ChatGPT.** Lean on its brainstorming strength to generate and evaluate structural options. "Give me three different ways to structure an article about X."
3. **Draft in Claude.** Take the best outline and your research to Claude. Give clear instructions about tone, audience, and length. Claude produces the draft.
4. **Review and edit in Claude.** Have Claude self-edit: "Review this draft for clarity, flow, and persuasiveness. Identify weak sections and suggest improvements."
5. **Final polish.** Do your own final pass. AI should handle the heavy lifting; the finishing touches are yours.

This workflow takes maybe 20% longer than using a single AI, but the output is substantially better. For important documents — anything client-facing, anything your name is on, anything going to executives — the extra effort pays off.

Common Writing Pitfalls Across Platforms

The AI Voice Problem

All AI writing has tells. Common ones to watch for and edit out:

- **"Delve"** — ChatGPT's favorite word. Replace with "explore," "examine," or just cut it.
- **"Tapestry"** and **"landscape"** — AI loves metaphors about weaving and terrain.
- **"It's worth noting that"** — a filler phrase that adds nothing. Delete it.
- **"In conclusion" at the start of a final paragraph** — AI treats every piece like a five-paragraph essay.
- **Excessive hedging** — "It may be argued that perhaps one could consider..." Just say what you mean.
- **Starting multiple paragraphs with "Moreover" or "Furthermore"** — a dead giveaway.

These show up across all platforms but most often in ChatGPT and least often in Claude.

The Over-Reliance Trap

AI should enhance your writing, not replace your voice. The best approach:

- Use AI for first drafts when you're staring at a blank page
- Use AI for editing when you have a draft but know it needs work
- Use AI for expansion when you have key points but need to develop them
- Use your own judgment for anything requiring real opinion, personal experience, or emotional honesty

No AI can write with your perspective, your experiences, or your understanding of your audience. The best AI-assisted writing happens when the AI does the structural heavy lifting and you bring the insight and personality.

The Bottom Line

For writing, Claude is the tool to beat. Not for every type of writing, and not for every stage of the process, but for overall prose quality, Claude produces work that needs the least editing and sounds the most human.

Use ChatGPT when you need energy, brainstorming, or short-form marketing copy. Use Gemini when you're working inside Google Docs and integration matters more than prose quality. Use Copilot when you're working inside Word and pulling from company data.

But when the quality of the writing itself is what matters — when you need prose that sounds like a skilled human wrote it — start with Claude.

Chapter 6: Research and Fact-Finding

If writing is the most common task people bring to AI, research is the most dangerous. When an AI makes up a source, invents a statistic, or confidently states something flat-out wrong, and you don't catch it, your credibility takes the hit. Not the AI's. Yours.

This chapter is about finding information you can actually trust. On that front, the platforms differ enormously.

The Trust Problem

The uncomfortable truth: most AI assistants will happily fabricate information. Not maliciously — they're language models generating plausible-sounding text, and a plausible-sounding citation looks the same to them as a real one.

I've personally caught: - ChatGPT citing journal articles that don't exist, with realistic titles, authors, and publication dates - Claude providing statistics that were directionally correct but numerically fabricated - Gemini attributing quotes to people who never said them - Copilot combining real facts in ways that produced a claim no source actually supports

This is why research is the one area where the choice of AI assistant isn't a preference — it's risk management.

Perplexity: The Research Champion

For research with citations, Perplexity isn't just the best option. It's in a different category.

How Perplexity Works Differently

Most AI assistants generate answers from their training data. When they cite sources, they're often reconstructing what a citation might look like rather than pointing to a real source they found.

Perplexity works fundamentally differently. For every query, it:

1. Searches the web in real time

2. Reads the actual pages it finds
3. Synthesizes the information from those pages
4. Provides inline citations that link directly to the sources it used

Every claim in a Perplexity response has a traceable source. Click the citation number, see the original page, and verify whether Perplexity represented what the source actually says.

What Perplexity Does Best

Current events and recent developments. Because Perplexity searches the web for every query, it has genuinely current information. "What happened in the AI industry this week?" gives you actual this-week information, not a summary from six months ago.

Factual questions with verifiable answers. "What is the current population of Tokyo?" "When was the last FDA approval for an Alzheimer's drug?" "What are the current interest rates?" These questions demand accuracy, and Perplexity delivers it with sources.

Comparative research. "Compare the privacy policies of the five major AI assistants" — Perplexity will actually read those privacy policies (or recent articles about them) and synthesize the comparison with citations.

Literature reviews. Perplexity's academic focus mode searches scholarly databases and provides properly formatted citations. As a starting point on academic research, it's genuinely useful.

Iterative investigation. Perplexity excels at follow-up questions. You can drill into a topic across multiple turns, and it holds context while searching for new information at each step.

Perplexity's Limitations for Research

Depth. Perplexity synthesizes and summarizes. It doesn't produce the deep, analytical prose you'd want in a research paper. Use it for finding information, not for writing about it.

Source quality. Perplexity searches the web broadly. It doesn't inherently distinguish between a peer-reviewed journal and a random blog post. You need to evaluate the sources it cites.

Nuance. For questions without clear factual answers — "Is remote work better than office work?" — Perplexity gives you a synthesis of what the web says, which can oversimplify genuinely complex debates.

Try This: The Citation Test

Ask both Perplexity and ChatGPT this question:

> "What percentage of companies have adopted AI tools as of 2025? Give me the specific statistic and the source."

Compare the results: - Does Perplexity give you a specific number with a clickable citation? (It should.) - Does ChatGPT give you a specific number? (It probably will.) Can you verify it? (Often you can't, or the source doesn't say quite what ChatGPT claims.)

Now click through Perplexity's citations. Does the source actually say what Perplexity claims? (Usually, but check.) This exercise alone will change how you think about AI-assisted research.

ChatGPT Browse: The Generalist Researcher

ChatGPT can browse the web and provide sources. It's not as research-focused as Perplexity, but far more capable than no web access at all.

Strengths

- **Conversational research.** You can hold a natural conversation where some questions need web searches and others don't, and ChatGPT handles the transitions smoothly.
- **Combining research with other tasks.** You can research a topic, then immediately ask ChatGPT to draft a memo based on what it found. Perplexity can't do this — it's a research tool, not a writing tool.
- **Image and media search.** ChatGPT can find and reference images, charts, and other media while browsing.

Weaknesses

- **Citation reliability.** ChatGPT's citations are less consistently accurate than Perplexity's. It sometimes cites pages that don't contain the claimed information, or synthesizes across sources in ways that introduce inaccuracies.

- **Selective searching.** ChatGPT doesn't always search the web when it should. It will answer from training data even when current information would serve you better, unless you explicitly say "search the web for this."
- **Source depth.** ChatGPT tends to cite fewer sources than Perplexity for the same query.

When to Use ChatGPT for Research

Use ChatGPT when you need to combine research with another task (writing, analysis, brainstorming) and the stakes are moderate. For a casual blog post, ChatGPT's web browsing is fine. For a report to your board, use Perplexity.

Gemini: The Google Search Advantage

Gemini has a unique advantage for research: it's backed by Google Search, the most comprehensive search engine in the world.

Strengths

- **Search quality.** When Gemini searches the web, it's using Google's index. No other AI has access to a better search engine for general web research.
- **Google ecosystem data.** Gemini can search your Gmail, Drive, and other Google services. "Find the email from last month about the Q2 budget" is something only Gemini can do.
- **Knowledge Graph integration.** For factual queries about entities — people, places, organizations — Gemini taps Google's Knowledge Graph, which is curated and generally reliable.
- **Maps and local information.** For location-based research, Gemini draws on Google Maps data.

Weaknesses

- **Citation format.** Gemini's citations are less prominent and less clickable than Perplexity's. It sometimes references sources without making them easy to verify.

- **AI Overviews habits.** Gemini falls into the same patterns as Google's AI Overviews — summarizing without sufficient attribution.
- **Mixing training data with search.** Like ChatGPT, Gemini blends training data with search results without clearly flagging which is which.

When to Use Gemini for Research

Use Gemini when your research involves your own Google data (emails, documents, calendar), when you need location-based information, or when you're already in the Google ecosystem and want to stay there.

Claude: The Analytical Researcher

Claude has web search, but it's not its primary strength. What Claude offers is a different research superpower: deep analysis of documents you provide.

Strengths

- **Document analysis.** Upload a 100-page PDF, a lengthy contract, a complex research paper, or several documents at once, and ask Claude to analyze them. Its 1M-token context window handles even book-length material.
- **Synthesis across documents.** Hand Claude five different sources and ask for a coherent summary. It's excellent at finding commonalities, contradictions, and gaps across multiple inputs.
- **Critical analysis.** Ask Claude to evaluate a study's methodology, identify weaknesses in an argument, or find logical gaps in a proposal. It's more genuinely analytical than ChatGPT, which tends to summarize without critiquing.
- **Honest uncertainty.** When Claude doesn't know something or isn't confident, it says so. Enormously valuable for research, where overconfidence is dangerous.

Weaknesses

- **Web search is not its strength.** Claude has limited web search, but it isn't designed as a research-first tool. For extensive current information, Perplexity or Gemini will serve you better.

- **Training data cutoff.** Claude's knowledge has a cutoff. For events after that cutoff, it simply won't have the information.

When to Use Claude for Research

Use Claude when your research involves analyzing documents you already have, when you need critical evaluation of sources, or when you want a thorough synthesis of multiple inputs. Think of Claude as the analyst who reviews your research, not the one who does the initial search.

The Multi-AI Research Workflow

For important research projects, the workflow that produces the most reliable results:

Step 1: Gather in Perplexity

Start your research in Perplexity. Ask your primary question. Follow up with more specific questions. Explore tangential topics that emerge. Bookmark or save the key sources.

Time: 10–15 minutes for a typical research question.

Step 2: Verify Key Claims

For the most important facts, statistics, and claims, click through Perplexity's citations and read the actual sources. Does the source say what Perplexity claims? Is the source itself credible?

Time: 5–10 minutes for spot-checking the most critical claims.

Step 3: Deep-Dive in Claude

Take your gathered research to Claude. Paste in the key findings, links, and any documents you're working with. Ask Claude to: - Identify gaps in your research - Flag any claims that look inconsistent or poorly supported - Synthesize the findings into a coherent narrative - Suggest angles you haven't considered

Time: 10–15 minutes.

Step 4: Cross-Check with Gemini (Optional)

For particularly important or contentious claims, ask Gemini the same questions. Different search engine, different model, different synthesis. If Perplexity and Gemini agree on a fact, you can be more confident. If they disagree, you've found something worth investigating.

Time: 5 minutes.

Total Time: 30–45 minutes for research you can stand behind.

Compare to the alternative: asking ChatGPT once, getting a confident-sounding answer with plausible-seeming citations, and using it without verification. That takes 5 minutes and creates significant risk of publishing inaccurate information.

Research Red Flags

Regardless of which AI you use, watch for these red flags:

Suspiciously specific statistics. "73.2% of companies adopted AI in 2025" — that level of specificity demands a source. If the AI can't produce one, the number is likely fabricated.

Perfect quotes. If an AI gives you a direct quote, verify it. AI models are especially prone to inventing plausible-sounding quotes that the person never actually said.

Dated information presented as current. The AI might hand you 2023 statistics when you asked about 2025. Always check the dates.

Circular sourcing. Sometimes an AI cites an article that itself used AI to generate content. You end up in a hall of mirrors.

Unanimous agreement where nuance exists. If you ask about a genuinely debated topic and the AI presents one side as settled fact, it's oversimplifying.

Try This: Build Your Research Stack

For the next week, every time you need to research something for work, use this approach:

1. Start in Perplexity
2. Take the findings to Claude for analysis
3. Note how long it takes and how confident you feel in the results

After a week, compare to your previous approach (probably asking one AI and hoping for the best). The difference in both quality and confidence is typically striking.

The Bottom Line

For research, the hierarchy is clear:

1. **Perplexity** for finding current, cited information
2. **Claude** for analyzing documents and synthesizing findings
3. **Gemini** for Google ecosystem integration and as a cross-check
4. **ChatGPT** for casual research combined with other tasks

Don't trust any AI for research without verification. But some make verification easier than others. Perplexity makes it easy. The others make you work for it.

Your credibility depends on the accuracy of your information. Use the tools that help you verify, not just the ones that help you find.

Chapter 7: Data Analysis and Spreadsheets

You have a spreadsheet. It has thousands of rows. Your boss wants to know the trends. You have a meeting in an hour.

This is exactly where the right AI assistant saves you from hours of manual work or a frantic scramble to remember pivot table syntax. The wrong AI wastes your time or, worse, gives you numbers that look right but aren't.

Data analysis is one of the areas where the gap between platforms is starkest. Some AIs actually run code on your data. Others only talk about what they'd do if they could. The distinction matters enormously.

The Fundamental Split: Execution vs. Advice

The most important thing to understand about AI data analysis is the difference between tools that *execute* code and tools that *suggest* code.

Tools that execute: ChatGPT (Advanced Data Analysis), Gemini (with code execution enabled) **Tools that suggest**: Claude (writes code but typically doesn't run it in the browser), Copilot (in standalone chat) **Tools that integrate**: Copilot in Excel, Gemini in Sheets (work inside the spreadsheet application itself)

This matters because data analysis requires iteration. You upload your data, ask a question, look at the result, realize you need to adjust the query, run it again. With an executing tool, this loop takes seconds. With a suggesting tool, you copy code to a terminal, run it, paste the output back — and the loop takes minutes.

ChatGPT: The Data Analysis Workhorse

ChatGPT's Advanced Data Analysis (renamed multiple times by OpenAI but functionally the same) is the gold standard for interactive data analysis in a chatbot.

How It Works

1. You upload a file (CSV, Excel, JSON, or others)
2. You describe what you want to know in plain English
3. ChatGPT writes Python code (using pandas, matplotlib, seaborn, etc.)
4. ChatGPT runs that code in a sandboxed environment
5. You get the results — tables, charts, numbers — right in the chat

The entire loop happens inside the conversation. No external tools needed.

What It Does Well

Exploratory analysis. "What are the main trends in this data?" ChatGPT inspects your columns, identifies numerical and categorical variables, generates summary statistics, and creates initial visualizations. It's like having a junior data analyst who works instantly.

Visualization. ChatGPT produces clean matplotlib and seaborn charts. Bar charts, line graphs, scatter plots, heatmaps, histograms — all from your natural-language description. Say "make the bars blue, add a title, and sort by descending value" and it updates the chart.

Data cleaning. "Remove rows with missing values in the revenue column," "convert the date column to datetime format," "merge these two sheets on the customer ID" — ChatGPT handles standard cleaning reliably.

Statistical tests. "Is there a statistically significant difference between Group A and Group B?" ChatGPT runs the appropriate test, shows the result, and explains what it means.

Downloadable outputs. Charts download as images. Cleaned datasets download as CSV or Excel files. Modified data stays available throughout the conversation.

Where It Falls Short

Large files. The sandbox has resource limits. Very large files (hundreds of megabytes) may cause timeouts or errors.

Complex multi-step analysis. For analysis that needs to maintain state across many steps (a multi-stage pipeline), the sandbox becomes unwieldy. Better to write the code properly in a development environment.

Reproducibility. ChatGPT's code is ephemeral — it lives in the sandbox during the conversation but isn't easily version-controlled or integrated into your codebase. Fine for one-off analysis. For recurring work, you need proper scripts.

Domain expertise. ChatGPT can run statistical tests, but it doesn't always pick the right test for your data distribution. For serious statistical work, you need enough statistics knowledge to verify it's using the right approach.

Try This: The Five-Minute Analysis

Take any CSV you have — sales data, survey results, website analytics, anything with a few columns and a few hundred rows. Upload it to ChatGPT and say:

> "Analyze this data. Give me: (1) summary statistics for all numerical columns, (2) any notable trends or patterns, (3) three visualizations that highlight the most interesting findings. Download links for the charts."

Time yourself. From upload to results, it should take under five minutes. Compare that to the same analysis done manually in Excel.

Gemini: The Google Sheets Native

Gemini handles data analysis two ways: through its standalone chat (with code execution) and through its Google Sheets integration.

Standalone Analysis

Gemini's code execution lets it run Python on uploaded data, similar to ChatGPT. The experience is functional but less polished:

- Code execution is reliable for straightforward tasks
- Visualizations are clean
- Natural-language understanding is good
- But the iterative loop isn't as smooth as ChatGPT's

Gemini in Google Sheets

This is where Gemini has a genuine, unique advantage. If your data lives in Google Sheets — and for many people, it does — you can use Gemini directly inside the spreadsheet:

- **Ask questions in natural language.** "What's the total revenue by region?" Gemini answers without you writing a formula.
- **Generate formulas.** "Create a formula that calculates the year-over-year growth rate" — Gemini writes and inserts the formula.
- **Create charts.** "Make a pie chart of sales by category" — done, right in your spreadsheet.
- **Data organization.** "Sort this by date and highlight cells where revenue exceeded $10,000" — Gemini handles conditional formatting and sorting.

Everything stays in the spreadsheet. No exporting, uploading, or downloading. Analysis and data live together.

When to Choose Gemini Over ChatGPT

- Your data is already in Google Sheets
- You want the analysis to remain in the spreadsheet, not in a chat
- You need to share the results with colleagues via Google Workspace
- You want formulas, not Python code

Copilot in Excel: The Enterprise Choice

Microsoft's Copilot in Excel brings AI analysis directly into the spreadsheet application that most enterprises use.

What It Does

- **Natural-language formulas.** "Calculate the average revenue per customer by quarter" — Copilot writes the Excel formula.
- **PivotTables.** "Create a pivot table showing sales by region and product category" — Copilot builds it.
- **Charts.** "Create a chart showing the trend of monthly revenue" — built and inserted into the spreadsheet.

- **Data insights.** "What are the notable patterns in this data?" — Copilot analyzes and describes trends.
- **Conditional formatting.** "Highlight all cells where the value decreased from the previous month" — done.

Strengths

- **No data leaves Excel.** For organizations with strict data governance, this matters. Your data doesn't get uploaded to a chatbot.
- **Enterprise integration.** Works with data in SharePoint, OneDrive, and across the Microsoft 365 ecosystem.
- **Formula creation.** For people who know what they want but can't remember the XLOOKUP syntax, Copilot is a godsend.

Weaknesses

- **Less flexible than Python.** Excel formulas can do a lot, but not everything a Python script can. For complex statistical analysis, transformations, or custom visualizations, ChatGPT's Python environment is more powerful.
- **Cost.** Microsoft 365 Copilot requires additional licensing beyond the base Office subscription.
- **Performance on large datasets.** Excel itself has performance limits on large datasets. Copilot doesn't fix that — it just makes it easier to write formulas that might still be slow.

When to Choose Copilot

- Your data is in Excel and needs to stay there
- Your organization uses Microsoft 365 and has Copilot licensing
- You need formulas and PivotTables, not Python scripts
- Data governance requires the analysis to stay within Microsoft's ecosystem

Claude: The Code Advisor

Claude doesn't run code in the browser (in its standard web interface). But Claude writes excellent data analysis code. The difference matters.

How to Use Claude for Data Analysis

A typical workflow:

1. Describe your data to Claude (or paste a sample of the first few rows)
2. Tell Claude what analysis you want
3. Claude writes clean, well-commented Python code
4. Copy the code and run it in your own environment (Jupyter, VS Code, terminal)
5. If the result isn't what you want, tell Claude and it adjusts the code

When This Approach Wins

Complex, multi-step analysis. When you need a proper pipeline — cleaning, transformation, analysis, visualization, all in a reproducible script — Claude writes better code than ChatGPT. Cleaner, better structured, better commented.

Production code. If the analysis needs to become a recurring report or part of your codebase, you want well-written code, not sandbox artifacts. Claude's data analysis code is production-quality.

Learning. If you want to understand the analysis, not just see the results, Claude's code is more educational. It explains what it's doing and why.

Claude Code. If you're using Claude Code (the terminal-based tool), Claude can execute Python on your machine. Best of both worlds: Claude's code quality with actual execution. Particularly powerful because Claude Code has access to your filesystem and can read your data files directly.

When This Approach Loses

Speed. The copy-paste-run loop is slower than ChatGPT's integrated execution.

Non-technical users. Without a Python environment set up, Claude's code suggestions aren't directly useful.

Iterative exploration. When you're exploring data and don't know what you're looking for yet, ChatGPT's fast sandbox feedback loop beats Claude's write-copy-run cycle.

Choosing Your Data Analysis Tool

Here's the decision tree:

Is the data in Google Sheets? - Yes → Use Gemini in Sheets

Is the data in Excel, and you need it to stay there? - Yes → Use Copilot in Excel

Do you need a quick, one-off analysis with visualizations? - Yes → Use ChatGPT Advanced Data Analysis

Do you need production-quality, reproducible analysis code? - Yes → Use Claude (or Claude Code)

Is the dataset very large (100MB+)? - Yes → Write code with Claude, run it locally where you have full computing resources

Common Data Analysis Tasks: Platform Comparison

Task	Best Tool	Why
"What are the trends?"	ChatGPT	Fast exploration with visuals
Generate Excel formulas	Copilot in Excel	Native integration
Generate Sheets formulas	Gemini in Sheets	Native integration
Create a chart from CSV	ChatGPT	Executes and renders immediately
Statistical hypothesis test	ChatGPT	Executes the test and explains results
Build a data pipeline	Claude	Best code quality and structure
Clean messy data	ChatGPT	Interactive cleaning with preview

Task	Best Tool	Why
Regular reporting script	Claude	Production-quality reproducible code
Analyze data in a presentation	Copilot in PowerPoint	Pulls data directly into slides

Try This: The Tool Comparison

Take the same CSV and analyze it in at least two platforms:

1. Upload it to ChatGPT and ask: "What are the three most important trends in this data? Show me visualizations."
2. Open it in Google Sheets and ask Gemini: "What are the notable patterns in this data?"

Compare: Which gave more useful insights? Which was faster? Which would you trust more?

If you have Excel and Copilot, try it there too. The comparison tells you which tool fits your workflow best — not in theory, in practice.

Data Privacy Considerations

A critical note: when you upload data to an AI assistant for analysis, you're sending it to the AI company's servers. For personal projects, this is usually fine. For company data — especially anything containing customer information, financial details, or proprietary metrics — check your organization's data policy before uploading.

- **ChatGPT Enterprise and Team** offer data isolation and no-training guarantees
- **Copilot in Excel** keeps data within the Microsoft 365 boundary (assuming your organization's data residency settings)
- **Gemini in Workspace** keeps data within the Google Workspace boundary
- **Claude** offers team and enterprise tiers with data protections

For sensitive data, the safest approach is often: have Claude write the analysis code, then run it locally on your own machine. The data never leaves your environment.

Chapter 15 covers data privacy across platforms in much more detail.

The Bottom Line

For most people, most of the time, ChatGPT's Advanced Data Analysis is the best tool for working with data. It's fast, it executes code, it produces visualizations, and it requires zero technical setup.

But "most of the time" isn't all the time. If your data lives in Google Sheets, use Gemini. If it lives in Excel, use Copilot. If you need production code, use Claude. If your data is sensitive, write code with Claude and run it locally.

The multi-AI advantage in data analysis is knowing which path to take — not just for the best results, but for the right results in the right place with the right security posture.

Chapter 8: Coding and Development

This chapter is for anyone who writes code — professionally or otherwise. Whether you're a senior software engineer, a data scientist, a hobbyist building side projects, or a business analyst who writes the occasional Python script, the AI landscape for coding has matured into something genuinely transformative.

But the tools differ enough that using the wrong one for the wrong task can cost you more time than it saves. Let me sort that out.

The Coding AI Landscape

As of early 2026, there are four major categories of AI coding tools:

1. **IDE-integrated assistants** (GitHub Copilot, Gemini Code Assist) — live inside your editor, provide inline suggestions as you type
2. **Terminal/CLI-based agents** (Claude Code) — operate from your terminal, can read your codebase, make multi-file changes, run commands
3. **Chat-based coding** (Claude.ai, ChatGPT, Gemini) — conversational coding in a browser, copy-paste workflow
4. **Specialized coding platforms** (Cursor, Windsurf, Replit) — purpose-built coding environments with AI deeply integrated

Each category excels at different things. Breaking them down:

GitHub Copilot: The Inline Completion King

GitHub Copilot is the most widely used AI coding tool in the world, and for good reason. It's embedded directly in your IDE — VS Code, JetBrains, Neovim — and provides code suggestions as you type.

What It Does Best

Autocomplete on steroids. Start typing a function, Copilot suggests the rest. Write a comment describing what you want, Copilot writes the code. Start a test, Copilot fills in the assertions. The suggestions are context-aware — they consider the file you're in, the imports you've made, the patterns in your codebase.

Boilerplate elimination. Database models, API endpoints, unit tests, data transformations — the repetitive structural code that makes up a significant portion of any codebase. Copilot handles this effortlessly. Write the first one, and it learns the pattern and generates the rest.

Language breadth. Copilot works well across dozens of languages. Python, JavaScript, TypeScript, Go, Rust, Java, C#, Ruby — whatever you're writing, Copilot has seen enough of it to help.

Copilot Chat. Beyond inline suggestions, GitHub Copilot includes a chat interface inside the IDE. Select code, ask "explain this," "find the bug," or "write tests for this function," and get responses right in your editor.

Where It Falls Short

Large-scale changes. Copilot operates at the level of suggestions within a single file. It's not designed to refactor across multiple files, restructure a project, or make architectural changes. For that, reach for a different tool.

Understanding the big picture. Copilot sees your current file and nearby files, but it doesn't deeply understand your codebase's architecture. It can suggest code that works in isolation but doesn't fit the broader pattern.

Novel or complex logic. For genuinely hard algorithmic problems or complex business logic, Copilot's suggestions are a starting point at best. It's great at pattern-matching but doesn't reason deeply about novel problems.

Debugging. Copilot can suggest fixes for simple bugs, but for complex debugging — the kind where you need to understand why something fails only under specific conditions — you need more context than Copilot's suggestion window provides.

Pricing

- Individual: $10/month or $100/year
- Business: $19/user/month
- Enterprise: $39/user/month

Best For

Day-to-day coding productivity. If you write code regularly, Copilot saves keystrokes on virtually every file you touch. The ROI is immediate and obvious.

Claude Code: The Codebase-Aware Agent

Claude Code is Anthropic's terminal-based coding assistant, and it represents a fundamentally different approach from inline completion. Instead of suggesting the next few lines, Claude Code operates as an autonomous agent that understands your entire codebase, makes multi-file changes, and executes commands.

What It Does Best

Codebase understanding. Claude Code reads and understands your entire project. Ask "how does the authentication system work?" and it traces through the relevant files, explains the flow, and points you to the key functions. Invaluable for unfamiliar codebases.

Multi-file changes. "Add a new API endpoint for user preferences, including the route, controller, model, migration, and tests." Claude Code creates or modifies files across your project, following the existing patterns. Inline completion tools fundamentally can't do this.

Refactoring. "Rename the User model to Account everywhere in the codebase." Claude Code handles this across all files, including tests, configuration, and documentation.

Greenfield development. When you're starting from scratch — a new feature, a new project, a new module — Claude Code scaffolds the structure and implements the initial version from your description.

Code review. Give Claude Code a diff or point it at a branch and ask for a review. You get substantive feedback on logic, patterns, potential bugs, and style.

Running and testing. Claude Code operates in your terminal, so it can run your tests, execute your build commands, and see the errors. When something fails, it reads the error, diagnoses the issue, and proposes a fix — all in one loop.

Where It Falls Short

Terminal-based. Claude Code runs in the terminal. If you prefer a graphical interface, the experience is less visual than IDE-based tools. (It integrates well with IDEs that have terminal panels.)

Speed for small edits. For quick one-line changes or simple autocomplete, Claude Code's agentic approach is overkill. You don't need an autonomous agent to write a for loop.

Cost of context. Because Claude Code reads your codebase to understand it, complex operations burn significant tokens. On large codebases, this adds up.

Pricing

Claude Code requires a Claude Pro ($20/month) or higher subscription. Token usage may be subject to rate limits depending on your plan.

Best For

Feature development, refactoring, codebase exploration, debugging complex issues, and any task that requires understanding code across multiple files.

ChatGPT for Coding

ChatGPT is a capable coding assistant in its chat interface, with the added advantage of executing Python code.

What It Does Best

Python execution. If you're working in Python, ChatGPT writes and runs the code in the chat. Upload a file, describe the script you need, and ChatGPT writes it, runs it, and shows the output. For data scripts, automation, and quick Python tasks, nothing's faster.

Explaining code. ChatGPT is excellent at explaining what existing code does. Paste in a complex function and ask "what does this do, line by line?" and you get a clear walkthrough.

Language translation. "Convert this Python function to JavaScript" or "rewrite this SQL query for PostgreSQL instead of MySQL" — ChatGPT handles language-to-language translation reliably.

Learning. If you're picking up coding or a new language/framework, ChatGPT's patient, detailed explanations are hard to beat.

Where It Falls Short

Code quality for production. ChatGPT's code works, but it isn't always well-structured. It writes functional code without great architecture — inline logic, thin error handling, limited edge-case thinking. Claude writes more production-ready code.

No codebase awareness. ChatGPT sees only what you paste into the chat. It can't read your project files or understand your architecture unless you tell it. For non-trivial projects, that means constant context-providing.

Copy-paste workflow. Unless you're using Python execution, the workflow is: describe → get code → copy to your editor → test → return to ChatGPT with errors → repeat. It works, but it's friction-heavy.

Best For

Python scripting, code explanation, learning, and quick one-off code tasks.

Gemini Code Assist

Google's coding AI, available in the IDE (VS Code, JetBrains, Android Studio) and through the Gemini chat interface.

What It Does Best

Android development. If you're building Android apps, Gemini Code Assist in Android Studio is purpose-built for it. It understands Android APIs, Material Design, and the Kotlin/Java ecosystem deeply.

Google Cloud integration. For code that runs on Google Cloud Platform, Gemini knows GCP services, configurations, and best practices.

Large context. Gemini's large context window lets it process more of your codebase than other chat-based tools when you paste in code.

Where It Falls Short

General coding quality. For general-purpose tasks, Gemini trails Claude and ChatGPT. Its suggestions are functional but less consistently excellent.

IDE integration polish. GitHub Copilot's VS Code integration is more polished. Gemini Code Assist works but feels like it's still catching up.

Best For

Android development, Google Cloud projects, and situations where you're already in the Google ecosystem.

Specialized Platforms: Cursor, Windsurf, Replit

A note on platforms that integrate AI at a deeper level:

Cursor is a fork of VS Code that puts AI at the center of the coding experience. It can reference your entire codebase, make multi-file edits, and uses various models (including Claude Opus 4.7, GPT-5.5, and Gemini 3.1 Pro) as backends. If you want IDE-level integration with agent-level capability, Cursor is worth trying.

Windsurf (formerly Codeium) offers a similar AI-first IDE experience with its own models and integrations.

Replit provides a browser-based coding environment with AI assistance. Especially useful for quick projects, prototyping, and collaborative coding.

These platforms blur the line between IDE and AI assistant. Worth evaluating if coding is your primary use case.

The Coding Decision Framework

Scenario	Best Tool	Why
Writing code line by line	GitHub Copilot	Fastest inline completion

Scenario	Best Tool	Why
Building a new feature (multiple files)	Claude Code	Multi-file awareness and execution
Quick Python script	ChatGPT	Write and run in one place
Understanding unfamiliar code	Claude Code	Reads and explains the whole codebase
Debugging a complex issue	Claude Code	Can run tests, read errors, iterate
Code review	Claude (chat or Code)	Thorough, architectural feedback
Explaining code to learn	ChatGPT	Patient, detailed explanations
Android development	Gemini Code Assist	Best Android-specific support
Generating boilerplate	GitHub Copilot	Pattern-matching at its best
Refactoring across files	Claude Code	Handles multi-file changes

The Multi-Tool Developer Workflow

Many developers I've talked to have settled on a two-tool approach:

GitHub Copilot + Claude Code. Copilot handles moment-to-moment typing — autocomplete, small functions, boilerplate. Claude Code handles the bigger tasks — new features, refactoring, debugging, code review. The two complement each other without much overlap.

This combination covers essentially all coding needs. Copilot at $10/month plus Claude Pro at $20/month is $30/month for an incredibly capable setup.

Some developers add ChatGPT for Python execution and data tasks, making it a three-tool stack. For most workflows, two tools are enough.

Try This: The Feature Test

Pick a small feature you've been meaning to build — something that touches at least two or three files. Try building it with Claude Code:

1. Describe the feature and your existing project structure
2. Let Claude Code scaffold the implementation
3. Review what it produces
4. Ask it to run the tests
5. Iterate on any issues

Time the entire process. Then consider how long the same feature would have taken with only inline autocomplete. The gap is usually measured in hours.

Common Coding Pitfalls

Trusting AI Code Without Reading It

The biggest mistake developers make with AI coding tools. AI-generated code often works but hides subtle issues:

- Security vulnerabilities (SQL injection, unsanitized input, hardcoded credentials)
- Performance problems (unnecessary database queries, missing indexes, O(n^2) algorithms)
- Missing error handling (happy path works, errors crash)
- Incorrect assumptions about your data or environment

Review AI-generated code as carefully as you'd review a junior developer's pull request.

Losing Your Skills

Accept every Copilot suggestion without thinking and you stop learning. You stop understanding your own codebase. When something breaks at 2 AM and you need to debug without AI, you need to actually understand the code.

Use AI to write code faster, not to replace your understanding.

Over-Describing to the Wrong Tool

Don't write three paragraphs of description to GitHub Copilot — it works on inline context, not long prompts. Conversely, don't try to use Copilot for a task that needs Claude Code's agentic capabilities. Match the description to the tool.

The Bottom Line

For coding, the landscape is genuinely excellent. GitHub Copilot makes every developer faster at the keystroke level. Claude Code makes complex tasks dramatically faster. ChatGPT handles Python execution and learning. Gemini serves the Google ecosystem.

The most productive developers in 2026 aren't using one tool — they're using two or three, each for what it does best. The investment is minimal ($30–50/month for a professional-grade AI coding stack), and the productivity gain is substantial.

If you write code for a living, you can't afford not to use these tools. And you can't afford to use only one of them.

Chapter 9: Creative Work

Creative work is where AI assistants diverge most dramatically. Some generate stunning images. Some can't generate images at all. Some produce creative writing that reads like literature. Some produce creative writing that reads like a press release trying to be fun.

This chapter covers the full spectrum of creative tasks — visual art, writing, audio, and video — and tells you which tool to reach for in each case.

Image Generation: The Current State

As of mid-2026, AI image generation has reached a level of quality that would have seemed impossible two years ago. Photorealistic images, consistent characters, readable text within images, and sophisticated style control are all achievable. But the capabilities vary wildly across platforms.

ChatGPT (Native Image Generation)

ChatGPT's image generation took a leap when OpenAI integrated generation directly into the model (starting with GPT-4o and carried forward into the GPT-5.x line) rather than treating it as a separate DALL-E tool. The results were transformative.

Strengths: - **Text in images.** ChatGPT can render readable text within images — signs, labels, book covers, memes. This was a notorious weakness of earlier models and the integrated approach handles it remarkably well. - **Conversational iteration.** Generate an image, then say "make the background more blue," "add a cat in the corner," or "change the text to say X." The model refines based on your feedback. - **Style range.** Photorealistic, cartoon, watercolor, pixel art, corporate, whimsical — the model handles a wide range of visual styles. - **Consistency.** Within a conversation, ChatGPT can hold visual consistency for a character or style across multiple generated images. Crucial for projects that need a coherent visual identity. - **Integration with text tasks.** Write a blog post and generate the header image in the same conversation. No switching tools.

Weaknesses: - **Rate limits.** On the Plus plan, you'll hit generation limits during heavy use. - **Hands and anatomy.** Dramatically improved, but AI image generation still occasionally produces anatomical oddities — though this is increasingly rare. - **Specific brand/person recreation.** ChatGPT has guardrails against generating images of real people and copyrighted characters.

Gemini (Imagen)

Google's Imagen models power Gemini's image generation.

Strengths: - Good photorealistic quality - Integration with Google products (generate images directly for Slides, Docs) - Competitive quality for most common image types

Weaknesses: - More conservative content policies than ChatGPT - Less reliable text rendering than ChatGPT's native generator - Fewer style options in practice

Claude

Claude cannot generate images. Full stop. If you need image generation, Claude is not the tool. Claude can analyze images you provide, describe them in detail, and write detailed image prompts for other tools. But it cannot create visual content.

This is Claude's biggest limitation for creative work. If your workflow requires both writing and image generation, pair Claude with another tool.

Copilot (Microsoft Designer)

Copilot integrates with Microsoft's image generation capabilities through Designer (formerly Bing Image Creator).

Strengths: - Free image generation included with Copilot - Integration with Microsoft 365 products - Good for presentation and document graphics

Weaknesses: - Less capable than ChatGPT's native generation - Fewer customization options - More limited style range

Standalone Image Tools

For serious creative work, dedicated platforms still beat chatbot-integrated generation:

Midjourney remains the quality leader for artistic image generation. Its aesthetic sense — particularly for illustration, concept art, and stylized photography — is ahead of chatbot-integrated tools. The tradeoff: it's a standalone tool (accessed through Discord or its web interface) with a separate subscription ($10–60/month).

Stable Diffusion offers open-source image generation that runs locally. Maximum control, maximum flexibility, zero privacy concerns. Requires technical setup and good hardware.

Adobe Firefly integrates AI generation into Photoshop and other Adobe tools. For professional designers already in the Adobe ecosystem, this is the most practical option.

The Image Generation Decision

Need	Best Tool	Why
Quick image for a document	ChatGPT	Fast, good quality, text-capable
Image for a presentation	Copilot (Office) or Gemini (Workspace)	Native integration
High-quality artistic image	Midjourney	Best aesthetic quality
Image with readable text	ChatGPT (native generator)	Best text rendering
Privacy-sensitive image creation	Stable Diffusion (local)	Data stays on your machine
Professional design work	Adobe Firefly	Integrates with design tools

Creative Writing

Creative writing deserves its own section because the platform differences are profound. This goes beyond the writing comparison in Chapter 5 — here we're talking fiction, poetry, screenwriting, songwriting, and other artistic text.

Claude: The Literary Writer

Claude produces the most literary creative writing of any major AI. Its fiction has voice, its characters feel three-dimensional, and its prose has rhythm. For:

- **Literary fiction**: Claude's default. Natural dialogue, atmospheric description, subtle character development.
- **Poetry**: Claude writes poetry that scans well and uses literary devices naturally, not mechanically.
- **Creative nonfiction**: Personal essays, memoir-style writing, narrative journalism — Claude handles personal voice well.
- **Screenwriting**: Claude understands screenplay format and writes natural-sounding dialogue with subtext.

Claude's limitation is that it can be too restrained. It pulls punches in dramatic scenes and adds unnecessary caveats to morally complex scenarios. You may need to push it: "Write the scene as intended. Don't soften it."

ChatGPT: The Genre Writer

ChatGPT excels at genre fiction and high-energy creative content:

- **Thriller/mystery**: ChatGPT writes compelling plot twists and suspenseful pacing.
- **Fantasy/sci-fi world-building**: Detailed, internally consistent worlds with rich lore.
- **Comedy**: ChatGPT is funnier than Claude. Its jokes land more often, and it's more willing to be irreverent.
- **Brainstorming**: "Give me ten plot ideas for a heist story set in a space station" — ChatGPT generates more varied options.

ChatGPT's limitation: its creative writing can feel performative. It leans on dramatic language, uses more exclamation points than necessary, and sometimes produces prose that reads like it's trying too hard.

Gemini: The Utility Writer

Gemini is serviceable for creative writing but doesn't excel at it. Use it when: - You need a quick creative exercise and don't want to switch tools - The writing is casual (social posts, witty messages) rather than ambitious - You're already in the Google ecosystem and convenience matters

Try This: The Story Opening

Give both Claude and ChatGPT this prompt:

> "Write the opening 500 words of a short story about a retired astronaut who discovers that the moon landing she participated in has been erased from all historical records. Write in first person, present tense. The tone should be unsettling but understated."

Compare: - Which one creates a more convincing character voice? - Which one handles "understated" better? (Hint: ChatGPT often overshoots into melodrama.) - Which opening would you actually want to keep reading?

Audio and Music

AI audio generation is evolving rapidly, though less integrated into the major chatbot platforms than text and image generation.

Voice and Speech

- **ChatGPT's Advanced Voice Mode** produces natural-sounding conversation with emotional range. It tells stories, performs characters, and holds genuinely engaging spoken exchanges.
- **ElevenLabs** leads AI voice cloning and text-to-speech. For voiceovers, narration, or audio content, it's the professional choice.
- **Google's text-to-speech** is strong, especially for multilingual content.

Music Generation

AI music generation is still emerging but advancing quickly:

- **Suno** and **Udio** generate complete songs from text descriptions — lyrics, melody, instrumentation. Quality is impressive for prototyping and casual use.
- None of the major chatbot platforms (ChatGPT, Claude, Gemini) generate music directly.

- For professional music production, AI tools are supplements (generating ideas, creating loops) rather than replacements.

Audio Decision Framework

Need	Best Tool
Voice conversation/storytelling	ChatGPT Advanced Voice
Professional voiceover	ElevenLabs
Song/music generation	Suno or Udio
Podcast editing assistance	Descript
Audio transcription	Whisper (OpenAI) or Google

Video

AI video generation made dramatic strides in 2025, but remains the least mature creative AI capability.

Current State

- **Sora (OpenAI)**: Generates short video clips from text prompts. Impressive for short clips but limited in duration and consistency.
- **Veo (Google)**: Google's video generation model, accessible through some Gemini integrations.
- **Runway**: An independent platform that's led AI video generation and editing.
- **Pika**: Another strong independent video generation platform.

Video Analysis (Not Generation)

For analyzing existing video, Gemini has a genuine lead: - Upload a video to Gemini and ask questions about it - Gemini identifies scenes, describes action, transcribes speech, and answers questions about video content - Useful for video review, content analysis, and accessibility

The Honest Assessment

AI video generation in mid-2026 is useful for short clips, B-roll, social media content, and prototyping. It's not yet capable of professional-quality long-form video. If you need professional video, AI is a tool in the process (for editing, effects, B-roll) rather than the whole process.

The Multi-AI Creative Workflow

Here's a workflow for a creative project that combines multiple AI strengths:

Example: Creating a blog post with original illustrations

1. **Research** in Perplexity — gather facts and inspiration
2. **Write** in Claude — draft the article with Claude's superior prose
3. **Generate images** in ChatGPT — create custom illustrations, header images, diagrams
4. **Create social cards** in ChatGPT — generate preview images for social media with text overlays
5. **Final review** in Claude — proofread and polish

Example: Creating a short story with audio narration

1. **Brainstorm** in ChatGPT — generate plot ideas and character concepts
2. **Write** in Claude — draft the story with literary quality
3. **Generate a cover image** in ChatGPT or Midjourney
4. **Create narration** in ElevenLabs — convert the text to spoken audio

Example: Building a presentation with visual flair

1. **Research** in Perplexity — gather data and talking points
2. **Outline** in Claude — structure the narrative
3. **Generate custom graphics** in ChatGPT — create diagrams, charts, and illustrations
4. **Build slides** in Copilot (PowerPoint) or Gemini (Slides) — assemble everything with proper formatting

Creative Ethics and Ownership

A quick but important note on the legal and ethical dimensions of AI-generated creative content:

Copyright. As of mid-2026, the legal status of AI-generated content is still evolving. In the United States, purely AI-generated images cannot be copyrighted (per the Copyright Office's current position). Works with substantial human creative input that incorporate AI-generated elements may qualify for protection. The law is still catching up.

Attribution. When using AI-generated images or text in published work, transparency is good practice. Not all contexts require disclosure, but professions and publications increasingly expect it.

Style mimicry. AI can imitate the style of specific artists. Whether you should ask it to is an ethical question worth considering. Many working artists have objected to their styles being replicated by AI.

Commercial use. Check each platform's terms of service for commercial use of generated content. Most paid tiers allow commercial use, but the specifics vary.

The Bottom Line

For creative work, the multi-AI approach isn't just helpful — it's almost mandatory, because no single platform covers all creative modalities:

- **Writing**: Claude for literary quality, ChatGPT for genre energy
- **Images**: ChatGPT for integrated generation, Midjourney for maximum quality
- **Audio**: ElevenLabs for voice, Suno for music
- **Video**: Still maturing; Gemini leads for analysis, Sora/Runway for generation

The creative professional's toolkit in 2026 is multi-platform by necessity. Embrace it. The combination of tools available today gives individual creators capabilities that would have required a full production team a few years ago.

Chapter 10: Business and Professional Use

This chapter is about the mundane work that eats your day: emails, meetings, presentations, reports, and the constant stream of professional communication that separates knowledge workers from the work they actually want to do. AI can take a massive bite out of this overhead — but only if you use the right tool for each piece.

Email: The Biggest Time Sink

The average knowledge worker spends over two hours a day on email. AI can cut that substantially, but the best approach depends on where your email lives.

Gmail Users: Gemini

If you use Gmail (personally or through Google Workspace), Gemini is your first choice for email assistance. Here's why:

Draft replies without context-switching. Gemini reads the email thread you're looking at and drafts a reply. No copy-paste into a chatbot and back. The draft appears right in Gmail.

Summarize long threads. A fifteen-email thread about a project decision? "Summarize this thread and identify the open questions" takes seconds with Gemini and saves you ten minutes of scrolling.

Tone adjustment. "Make this reply more diplomatic" or "make this more concise" — quick inline edits without leaving the email.

Search across your inbox. "Find the email from Sarah about the Q3 budget from last month" — Gemini searches your Gmail and finds what you need faster than manual searching.

Outlook Users: Copilot

If you use Outlook (especially in a Microsoft 365 business environment), Copilot is the equivalent tool:

Draft from context. Copilot reads the email thread and drafts a response. It also pulls in information from your calendar, other emails, and shared documents.

Meeting prep. "Summarize my emails with this client from the last two weeks" — Copilot synthesizes the communication history before a meeting.

Follow-up reminders. Copilot identifies emails that need responses and drafts follow-ups.

Standalone AI for Emails

For emails that need more careful crafting — a negotiation, a sensitive message, a client proposal — the in-app assistants may not be enough:

Use Claude to draft the email. Give it the context (situation, recipient, desired outcome) and let it produce a draft with appropriate tone and structure. Then paste it into your email client.

Use ChatGPT if you want options. "Give me three versions of this email: one formal, one friendly, one direct." ChatGPT's brainstorming strength works well for finding the right approach.

Try This: The Email Speed Test

For one week, use AI for every email that takes more than two minutes to draft. Track the time you save. Most people save 30–60 minutes per day — 2.5–5 hours per week, or roughly a full work month per year.

Meetings: Before, During, and After

AI's impact on meetings is one of the most underappreciated productivity gains available.

Before the Meeting: Preparation

Copilot in Teams summarizes previous meetings with the same participants, surfaces relevant emails and documents, and prepares you for what's coming. "What did we agree to in last month's project review?" is a quick question instead of a fifteen-minute document search.

Gemini in Google Meet offers similar preparation for Google Workspace users.

Claude or ChatGPT help prepare for meetings that need more thoughtful preparation. Give them the agenda, the key participants, and what you want to accomplish, and ask for talking points, potential objections, and strategic recommendations.

During the Meeting: Real-Time Assistance

Copilot in Teams and **Gemini in Google Meet** both provide real-time meeting assistance: - Automatic transcription - Real-time summaries - Action item identification - Catching up if you join late ("What have I missed?")

Both require the meeting to be recorded and the feature enabled. Both work best in their native platforms.

For in-person meetings or meetings on other platforms, tools like Otter.ai, Fireflies.ai, or Granola provide AI-powered transcription and summarization.

After the Meeting: Follow-Up

This is where AI saves the most meeting-related time:

Copilot generates meeting summaries in Teams with action items, decisions, and follow-ups. Share them directly with attendees.

Gemini does the same in Google Meet, with the summary stored in Google Docs.

Claude is excellent for turning meeting notes into structured deliverables. Hand it the raw transcript or summary: "Turn these meeting notes into (1) a summary email for the team, (2) a list of action items with owners and deadlines, and (3) an agenda for the follow-up meeting." Claude handles structured transformation beautifully.

Presentations: Slides That Don't Take Hours

Building presentations is one of the most time-consuming professional tasks. AI changes the equation.

Copilot in PowerPoint

If you use PowerPoint, Copilot can:

- **Generate a presentation from a document.** Give it a Word document, a report, or even a prompt, and it creates a slide deck with appropriate layouts, content, and formatting.
- **Follow your company template.** It works within your organization's branded templates.
- **Add specific slides.** "Add a slide comparing Q1 and Q2 revenue" — it creates the slide with the right chart type.
- **Redesign existing slides.** "Make this slide more visual" — it restructures the layout.
- **Speaker notes.** It can generate speaker notes for each slide.

Gemini in Google Slides

Gemini offers similar capabilities within Google Slides: - Generate presentations from prompts or documents - Create individual slides on specific topics - Generate images for slides - Suggest layouts and designs

The Hybrid Approach

For presentations that really matter — board decks, investor pitches, major client proposals — the best approach uses multiple tools:

1. **Outline in Claude.** Give Claude the objective, audience, and key messages. Its structured thinking produces the best narrative flow for presentations. "Create a 12-slide outline for a board presentation on our 2026 strategy. The key themes are..."

2. **Research in Perplexity.** For slides that need current data, competitive analysis, or market information, gather it from Perplexity with citations.

3. **Build in Copilot/Gemini.** Take the outline and research to your native presentation tool. Let the AI assistant build the initial deck.
4. **Generate custom visuals in ChatGPT.** For slides that need custom graphics, diagrams, or illustrations, generate them in ChatGPT and insert them into the deck.
5. **Refine manually.** The AI gets you 70% of the way. The last 30% — adjusting layouts, perfecting wording, making sure the story flows — is human work.

This workflow produces a solid presentation in an hour that would have taken four hours without AI.

Reports and Documents

Professional reports — quarterly reviews, market analyses, project updates, white papers — are another area where multi-AI workflows shine.

Short Reports (1–5 pages)

For shorter reports, a single AI is usually sufficient:

Claude for reports that need nuanced analysis and polished writing. Output reads like an experienced analyst wrote it.

ChatGPT for reports that need data visualization. If the report is numbers-heavy, ChatGPT both analyzes the data and produces the charts.

Copilot for reports that need to pull from Microsoft 365 data sources — SharePoint documents, Excel files, Teams conversations.

Long Reports (10+ pages)

For longer documents, a multi-AI approach pays off:

1. **Structure in Claude.** Create a detailed outline with section descriptions.
2. **Research in Perplexity.** Gather data for each section.
3. **Draft in Claude.** Write the report section by section, providing research findings for each.
4. **Analyze data in ChatGPT.** Generate charts and statistical analysis.

5. **Review in Claude.** Use Claude to review the completed draft for consistency, gaps, and quality.

Try This: The Report Accelerator

Take a report you need to write this week. Before you start, spend fifteen minutes creating a detailed outline in Claude:

> "I need to write a [type] report about [topic]. The audience is [who]. The key sections should cover [what]. Create a detailed outline with descriptions of what each section should contain, what data I need for each section, and the key argument or finding each section should present."

Use that outline as your roadmap. A well-structured outline makes the actual writing dramatically faster, whether you write it yourself or use AI for drafting.

Professional Communication Beyond Email

Slack and Teams Messages

For internal communication platforms:

Claude in Slack (where deployed) summarizes channels, drafts messages, and answers questions about your workspace's content.

Copilot in Teams provides similar capabilities: channel summaries, message drafting, and conversation search.

For important Slack/Teams messages (announcements, sensitive communications), draft them in Claude or ChatGPT first. Internal messages feel casual, but the important ones deserve the same care as email.

Client Communication

Client-facing communication demands extra care:

- **Proposals**: Outline in Claude, research in Perplexity, final draft in Claude
- **Status updates**: Copilot or Gemini for pulling data from your project tools; Claude for crafting the narrative

- **Difficult conversations**: Claude for drafting sensitive messages. Its nuance with tone matters here.

Social Media and Public Communication

For company social media and public-facing content:

- **LinkedIn posts**: ChatGPT tends to write the most "LinkedIn-native" content (for better or worse)
- **Twitter/X**: ChatGPT for punchy, concise posts
- **Blog posts**: Claude for substantive content
- **Press releases**: Claude for the initial draft (more measured tone), ChatGPT for the headline (more attention-grabbing)

The Business Professional's Daily AI Stack

Here's what a typical day looks like for a business professional with an optimized AI toolkit:

8:00 AM — Open Copilot in Teams or Gemini in Workspace. Review meeting summaries from yesterday. Identify follow-ups.

8:30 AM — Use Copilot/Gemini to draft responses to routine emails.

9:00 AM — For the important email that requires careful framing, draft it in Claude.

10:00 AM — Meeting with automatic AI transcription. Catch up on anything missed.

11:00 AM — Use Perplexity to research a competitor mentioned in the meeting.

11:30 AM — Draft a brief strategy memo in Claude based on the meeting discussion and research.

1:00 PM — Use ChatGPT to analyze the sales data that was discussed in the morning meeting.

2:00 PM — Build presentation slides using Copilot/Gemini with the analysis and memo.

3:00 PM — Share the meeting summary (auto-generated) and the strategy memo with the team.

4:00 PM — Use Copilot/Gemini to draft tomorrow's meeting agendas based on today's follow-ups.

Total AI interactions: 8–10. Time saved versus the pre-AI workflow: an estimated 2–3 hours. That's not a small number. Over a year, it's 500–750 hours — roughly three to four months of working time.

The ROI Calculation

For business professionals, AI subscriptions pay for themselves quickly:

- Claude Pro: $20/month
- Copilot or Gemini: $20/month (or included in your organization's licensing)
- Total: $20–40/month

If AI saves you even one hour per week (a conservative estimate), and your time is worth $50–200/hour, the ROI is 5x–40x. For most professionals, the real savings are much larger.

The Bottom Line

Business and professional use is where the multi-AI approach delivers its most tangible returns. Not because any single task is revolutionary, but because small time savings across dozens of daily tasks compound into hours.

Use your ecosystem's native AI (Copilot or Gemini) for integration-heavy tasks. Use Claude for anything that needs careful writing or thinking. Use ChatGPT for data and visuals. Use Perplexity when you need facts.

Professionals who adopt this multi-tool approach don't just save time — they produce better work. Their emails are more thoughtful. Their presentations are more polished. Their reports are better researched. And they leave the office earlier.

That's the real payoff.

Chapter 11: Education and Learning

Whether you're a student trying to understand organic chemistry, a professional learning a new programming language, or a lifelong learner exploring history for the sheer joy of it, AI assistants have fundamentally changed what it means to study. You have access to an infinitely patient tutor who knows virtually every subject, is available at 3 AM, and never makes you feel dumb for asking a basic question.

But not all AI tutors are equal. And how you use them matters as much as which one you choose.

AI as a Learning Tool: The Paradigm Shift

Before we compare platforms, let's address the elephant in the room: AI can help you learn, or it can do your learning for you. These are opposite outcomes.

Paste an essay prompt into ChatGPT, copy the output, and submit it, and you've learned nothing. Use ChatGPT to explain a concept you're struggling with, then write the essay yourself with that understanding, and you've learned a lot. Same tool, completely different outcomes.

This chapter assumes you want to learn, not just get answers. With that goal in mind, some AI assistants are significantly better learning tools than others.

The Tutor Comparison

ChatGPT: The Patient Explainer

ChatGPT excels as a tutor for several reasons:

Multiple explanation styles. "Explain this like I'm five." "Now explain it like I'm a college student." "Now explain it with a sports analogy." ChatGPT adapts fluidly and doesn't tire of being asked to try again.

Step-by-step walkthroughs. For math, science, and technical subjects, ChatGPT works through problems step by step, showing its reasoning at each stage. Say "I don't understand step 3, explain that more" and it zooms in without losing the broader context.

Enthusiasm. ChatGPT's eager-to-please personality, annoying in professional contexts, is a strength for learning. It's encouraging without being condescending. It celebrates when you get things right.

Visual aids. ChatGPT generates diagrams, charts, and illustrations to support explanations. "Draw a diagram of the water cycle" produces a visual you can study.

Code execution for STEM. For subjects involving math, statistics, or programming, ChatGPT runs code to demonstrate concepts. "Show me what happens to a sine wave when you increase the frequency" — it generates the plot.

Claude: The Deep Thinker

Claude approaches tutoring differently, and for certain kinds of learning, it's the better choice:

Nuanced explanations. Claude excels when a subject requires nuance and doesn't have simple right-or-wrong answers. Philosophy, literature analysis, ethics, political theory, complex historical causation — Claude handles ambiguity and multiple perspectives better than ChatGPT.

Socratic method. Tell Claude to "teach me by asking questions rather than giving answers," and it becomes an excellent Socratic tutor. It asks probing questions that guide you to understanding rather than handing you conclusions.

Writing feedback. For learning to write better, Claude gives the most useful feedback. It identifies specific weaknesses, explains why they're weaknesses, and suggests improvements without rewriting everything for you.

Honest assessment. If your understanding is wrong, Claude is more likely to say so directly. ChatGPT sometimes validates incorrect reasoning to avoid seeming harsh.

Reading comprehension. Upload a text to Claude and discuss it. Claude's analysis of literature, academic papers, and complex documents is deeper and more insightful than other platforms.

Gemini: The Google Scholar

Gemini has specific advantages for academic learning:

Google Scholar integration. For academic topics, Gemini taps Google Scholar, providing peer-reviewed sources directly in the conversation.

YouTube integration. For visual learners, Gemini references and summarizes educational YouTube videos on the topic you're studying.

Multimodal learning. Upload a textbook page, a diagram, or a photo of your notes, and Gemini explains what it sees. For subjects with visual components (anatomy, geography, art history), this is valuable.

Very large context. Gemini's massive context window lets you upload entire chapters or textbooks for discussion. "Here's the chapter on thermodynamics. Help me understand the second law."

Perplexity: The Fact-Checker

Perplexity's role in learning is specific but important:

Verifying claims. When ChatGPT or Claude explains something and you're not sure it's right, check it in Perplexity. You'll get the answer with sources you can verify.

Finding primary sources. "Find the original paper that proposed the theory of plate tectonics" — Perplexity locates it, with the citation.

Current information for evolving subjects. For fields that change rapidly — technology, medicine, law, current events — Perplexity keeps you on current information, not outdated training data.

Learning Use Cases: Platform Recommendations

Studying for Exams

Best approach: ChatGPT + Claude

Use ChatGPT for: - Generating practice questions: "Give me 20 multiple-choice questions on cellular biology at the AP Biology level" - Step-by-step problem solving in math and science - Quick concept explanations - Flashcard generation: "Create 30 flashcard pairs for these vocabulary terms"

Use Claude for: - Reviewing your essay drafts before submission - Understanding complex texts (upload the reading and discuss it) - Preparing for essay exams (Claude challenges your arguments and helps you strengthen them) - Subjects that require synthesis and critical thinking

Try This: The Study Session

Pick a subject you're studying or want to learn. Open two windows: Claude and ChatGPT.

Start with ChatGPT: "I'm studying [subject]. Test my knowledge by asking me five increasingly difficult questions. After each answer, tell me if I'm right and explain the correct answer."

Then switch to Claude: "I'm studying [subject]. I think I understand the following concept: [explain your understanding]. Critique my understanding — what am I getting right, what am I getting wrong, and what am I missing?"

This two-AI study session covers both breadth (ChatGPT testing your knowledge across topics) and depth (Claude probing the quality of your understanding).

Learning a New Language

AI language tutoring has become remarkably effective:

ChatGPT with Advanced Voice Mode is the best for conversational practice. You can have spoken conversations in the target language, and ChatGPT gently corrects your grammar and suggests better phrasing. It's a patient conversation partner available 24/7.

Claude is better for grammar rules, reading comprehension in the target language, and detailed explanations of why something is said a particular way.

Gemini is useful for translation practice and Google Translate integration.

Best multi-AI workflow: 1. Study grammar concepts in Claude (deep understanding) 2. Practice conversation in ChatGPT Voice (spoken fluency) 3. Verify translations and idioms in Perplexity (accuracy)

Learning to Code

This overlaps with Chapter 8, but from a learning perspective:

ChatGPT is the best tutor for coding beginners. Patient explanations, step-by-step concepts, and code execution to show you the results. "Explain Python lists with five examples, starting with the simplest" gets you a progressive learning experience.

Claude is better for intermediate learners who need to understand why code works the way it does, not just what to type. Claude explains underlying concepts — memory management, design patterns, algorithmic complexity — more deeply.

GitHub Copilot is not a learning tool. It writes code for you. If you're trying to learn, turn it off, write the code yourself, then compare with what Copilot would have suggested.

Professional Development

For learning new professional skills — project management, data analysis, negotiation, public speaking:

Claude excels at scenario-based learning. "Act as a difficult client who's unhappy with the project timeline. Let me practice the conversation." Claude creates realistic scenarios with genuine pushback.

ChatGPT excels at structured curricula. "Create a 4-week self-study plan for learning financial modeling." Organized, progressive learning plans.

Perplexity finds the best resources. "What are the most recommended books and courses for learning UX design in 2026?" Current recommendations with sources.

Research for Academic Papers

For students and researchers writing academic papers:

1. **Start in Perplexity** — Literature search, finding key papers and their citations
2. **Analyze sources in Claude** — Upload papers, discuss methodology, identify gaps

3. **Draft in Claude** — Academic writing is Claude's strength
4. **Verify facts in Perplexity** — Cross-check any claims before finalizing
5. **Generate data visualizations in ChatGPT** — For papers that include data analysis

AI and Academic Integrity

Let's be direct about this. Every educational institution is grappling with AI, and the rules vary. Some key principles:

Know your institution's policy. Before using AI for any academic work, understand what your school, university, or program allows. Policies range from "no AI ever" to "AI is encouraged with disclosure."

Disclose when required. If you used AI to help with an assignment, say so. Many institutions have specific disclosure requirements.

Use AI to learn, not to bypass learning. There's a bright line between "I used Claude to help me understand the concept, then wrote the essay myself" and "I pasted the prompt into Claude and submitted what it wrote." The first is studying. The second is academic dishonesty.

AI-generated work is detectable — sometimes. Detection tools exist but are unreliable. They produce both false positives (flagging human-written work as AI) and false negatives (missing AI-generated work). Don't rely on detection tools to protect you, and don't assume you won't get caught.

The real cost of cheating is to yourself. Bypass learning now, and you'll lack the knowledge later when it matters. The essay doesn't matter. What you learn writing it does.

For Educators: Using AI in Teaching

If you're an educator, AI can enhance your teaching:

Creating materials: - Use ChatGPT to generate practice problems at specific difficulty levels - Use Claude to create discussion questions that probe deep understanding - Use ChatGPT to generate images and visual aids

Differentiated instruction: - Create explanations at multiple levels for the same concept - Generate modified assignments for different learning needs - Create rubrics and assessment criteria

Feedback: - Use Claude to help draft detailed feedback on student work (but always add your own observations) - Use ChatGPT to identify common error patterns across a class

Stay current: - Use Perplexity to stay updated on the latest developments in your field - Use Claude to explore new pedagogical approaches

Try This: The Lesson Plan

If you're an educator, try this:

> Give Claude: "I'm teaching [subject] to [level] students. The topic is [specific topic]. Create a lesson plan that includes: (1) a hook to engage students, (2) three activities that build understanding progressively, (3) a formative assessment, and (4) a discussion question that requires critical thinking."

Compare what Claude produces with your existing lesson plan. You'll likely find elements worth incorporating.

Specialized Learning Tools

Beyond the major platforms, several specialized tools deserve mention:

Khan Academy's Khanmigo — An AI tutor built for education, with guardrails designed for student learning. It won't give answers directly; instead, it guides students to discover answers themselves.

Duolingo — Uses AI for personalized language learning with gamification.

Wolfram Alpha — For math and science, Wolfram Alpha provides computational answers and step-by-step solutions. It complements AI chatbots because it computes rather than predicts.

Quizlet — AI-enhanced flashcard and study tools.

These specialized tools often outperform general-purpose AI assistants in their domains because they're designed for learning outcomes, not just answer generation.

Building a Personal Learning Stack

Here's the learning stack I recommend:

1. **Primary tutor: ChatGPT** — for explanations, practice problems, and interactive learning
2. **Depth check: Claude** — for nuanced understanding, writing feedback, and critical analysis
3. **Fact verification: Perplexity** — for checking claims and finding sources
4. **Study materials: ChatGPT** — for flashcards, quizzes, and study plans
5. **Conversation practice: ChatGPT Voice** — for language learning and verbal skills

Total cost: ChatGPT Plus ($20/month) + Claude free tier for occasional deep discussions + Perplexity free tier for verification = $20/month for a comprehensive learning toolkit.

The Bottom Line

AI has democratized access to expert tutoring. A student in a rural area with limited access to tutors now has 24/7 access to an AI that can explain quantum physics, critique an essay, practice French conversation, or generate AP-level practice exams.

The key is using AI to enhance learning, not replace it. The student who uses AI as a study partner outperforms the one who uses it as a homework machine. The professional who uses AI to accelerate skill development outperforms the one who uses it to avoid learning.

Use ChatGPT for broad, interactive learning. Use Claude for depth and critical thinking. Use Perplexity for verification. And always do the thinking yourself. AI is the best study partner you've ever had — but a study partner who does all the work isn't helping you learn.

Part III: Multi-AI Workflows

"Coming together is a beginning, staying together is progress, and working together is success."

— Henry Ford (attributed)

Chapter 12: Multi-AI Workflows

This is the chapter that separates people who use AI from people who are genuinely good at it. Everything before this was about picking the right tool for a task. This chapter is about chaining multiple tools together for results no single AI can achieve alone.

If the previous chapters taught you which wrench to grab, this chapter teaches you how to build the engine.

What Is a Multi-AI Workflow?

A multi-AI workflow is a deliberate sequence of steps across multiple AI assistants, where the output of one step becomes the input for the next. Each AI handles the part it's best at, and the final result beats what any single AI could produce alone.

This isn't about asking multiple AIs the same question and picking the best answer (though that's useful too). It's about designing a process where each AI contributes its unique strength to a larger outcome.

Here's a simple example:

Goal: Produce a well-researched, well-written article about renewable energy trends in 2026.

Single-AI approach: Ask ChatGPT to write the article. You get an okay article with unverified claims.

Multi-AI workflow: 1. **Perplexity**: Research current renewable energy trends. Get cited statistics and recent developments. 2. **Claude**: Draft the article from the research. Polished, human-sounding prose. 3. **ChatGPT**: Generate a custom header image for the article. 4. **Claude**: Final proofread and quality check.

The second approach takes maybe 20% more time but produces output dramatically better in accuracy, writing quality, and visual presentation.

The Core Workflow Patterns

After building and testing dozens of multi-AI workflows, I've identified five fundamental patterns that cover most cases:

Pattern 1: Research-Write-Polish

The sequence: Perplexity → Claude → Claude (self-edit) or ChatGPT (visual elements)

Best for: Any content that needs to be both accurate and well-written.

How it works: 1. Use Perplexity to gather information with citations 2. Take the key findings to Claude with instructions for the final piece 3. Have Claude (or yourself) do a final review pass 4. If the piece needs images, generate them in ChatGPT

Example: A blog post comparing cloud storage providers. - Perplexity: "What are the current pricing, features, and limitations of Dropbox, Google Drive, OneDrive, and iCloud as of 2026? Include specific pricing tiers and storage limits." - Claude: "Using the following research [paste Perplexity's findings], write a 2,000-word comparison article for a tech-savvy but non-technical audience. Be honest about trade-offs. Include a recommendation." - ChatGPT: "Generate a comparison infographic showing the four cloud storage providers with their logos, pricing, and key features."

Pattern 2: Brainstorm-Evaluate-Develop

The sequence: ChatGPT → Claude → Claude or ChatGPT (execution)

Best for: Creative projects, strategy development, problem-solving.

How it works: 1. Use ChatGPT to generate many options (more creatively prolific) 2. Use Claude to evaluate the options (more critically honest) 3. Use whichever AI is best suited for developing the winning idea

Example: Naming a new product. - ChatGPT: "Generate 30 possible names for a project management app aimed at creative agencies. Include a mix of abstract, descriptive, and playful options." - Claude: "Here are 30 candidate names for a project management app for creative agencies. [Paste list.] Evaluate each name on: memorability, domain name availability likelihood, trademark risk, appeal to creative professionals, and international pronunciation. Recommend the top 5 with reasoning." - ChatGPT: "For the name [winning name], generate a logo concept, a tagline, and a 100-word product description."

Pattern 3: Analyze-Visualize-Present

The sequence: ChatGPT (data analysis) → Claude (narrative) → Copilot/Gemini (presentation)

Best for: Business presentations, reports that combine data with storytelling.

How it works: 1. Use ChatGPT to analyze data and generate visualizations 2. Use Claude to write the narrative that explains the data 3. Use Copilot or Gemini to assemble the presentation in your suite

Example: Quarterly business review. - ChatGPT: Upload the quarterly data. "Analyze this data and create visualizations showing: (1) revenue trends by product line, (2) customer acquisition cost over time, (3) top 5 performing regions. Download all charts." - Claude: "Based on these findings [describe the data highlights], write the narrative for a quarterly business review. The audience is the executive team. Highlight the positive trends but be honest about areas of concern. Suggest three strategic recommendations based on the data." - Copilot in PowerPoint: "Create a 15-slide quarterly business review using this outline [paste Claude's narrative]. Insert these charts [upload ChatGPT's visualizations]."

Pattern 4: Draft-Critique-Revise

The sequence: Claude → ChatGPT (or Claude with a critique prompt) → Claude

Best for: Any important document that needs to be as good as possible.

How it works: 1. Use Claude to write the initial draft 2. Use a second AI (or Claude with a different prompt) to critique it 3. Use Claude to revise based on the critique

Example: A grant proposal. - Claude: "Draft a grant proposal for [describe the project, funding agency, requirements]." - ChatGPT: "You are a harsh but fair grant reviewer for [funding agency]. Review this proposal. Identify weaknesses in the methodology, gaps in the literature review, unclear objectives, and any section that doesn't meet [funding agency's] typical standards. Be specific and constructive." - Claude: "Here is a draft grant proposal [paste original] and here is the reviewer feedback [paste critique]. Revise the proposal to address every point of feedback while maintaining the original goals and structure."

This pattern produces significantly better output than any single pass, no matter which AI you use.

Pattern 5: Multi-Source Synthesis

The sequence: Perplexity + Gemini (parallel research) → Claude (synthesis) → ChatGPT (verification)

Best for: Important research where accuracy is critical and no single source is sufficient.

How it works: 1. Research the same question in both Perplexity and Gemini (different search engines, different models) 2. Take both sets of findings to Claude for synthesis 3. Use ChatGPT to cross-check any claims that seem uncertain

Example: Market analysis for a business decision. - Perplexity: "What is the current market size and growth rate of the electric vehicle charging industry in North America?" - Gemini: Same question (uses Google Search, may find different sources) - Claude: "Here are two sets of research findings on the EV charging market. [Paste both.] Synthesize these into a coherent market analysis. Note where the sources agree, where they disagree, and what the most reliable consensus view appears to be." - ChatGPT: "Verify this claim: [any specific statistic you want to double-check]. Search the web for the original source."

Building Your Own Workflows

The five patterns above are starting points. The real power comes from adapting them to your specific work. Here's how to design one:

Step 1: Define the Output

What do you need at the end? A document? A presentation? A decision? A plan? Start with the deliverable.

Step 2: Identify the Capabilities Needed

What skills does the deliverable require? Research? Writing? Data analysis? Visual design? Critical evaluation? List them.

Step 3: Match Capabilities to Tools

For each capability, which AI does it best? - Research → Perplexity - Writing → Claude - Data analysis → ChatGPT - Visuals → ChatGPT - Presentation assembly → Copilot/Gemini - Critical evaluation → Claude - Brainstorming → ChatGPT

Step 4: Design the Sequence

In what order should the steps happen? Generally: 1. Research comes first (you need facts before you can write) 2. Analysis comes before writing (understand the data before explaining it) 3. Brainstorming comes before evaluation (generate before you filter) 4. Writing comes before editing (obvious) 5. Visual creation can run in parallel with writing

Step 5: Define the Handoff Points

What information needs to pass from one AI to the next? This is the critical step. Bad handoffs waste the work you did in the previous step. Good ones preserve context and set up the next step for success.

A good handoff includes: - The key findings or output from the previous step - The context the next AI needs (audience, format) - Specific instructions for the next step - Any constraints or requirements

Handoff Best Practices

The handoff between AIs is where most multi-AI workflows break down. Here's how to do it well:

Carry Context, Not Just Content

Bad handoff: Copy-paste the raw output from Perplexity into Claude.

Good handoff: "I researched [topic] and found the following key points: [summarize, don't dump]. Sources: [list key sources]. Using this research, write a [format] for [audience]. The tone should be [tone]. The key message is [message]."

Summarize When Crossing AI Boundaries

Different AIs have different context windows and different strengths. When moving between them, summarize the key points rather than transferring massive blocks of text. It also helps you verify the work — if you can't summarize what the first AI found, you might not have understood it well enough.

Preserve Citations

When research moves from Perplexity (which cites everything) to Claude (which writes prose), explicitly tell Claude to preserve the citations: "Include inline citations from the research in the final draft."

Reset Tone Expectations

Different AIs have different default tones. When moving from ChatGPT (enthusiastic) to Claude (measured), include tone instructions to avoid jarring inconsistencies.

Try This: Your First Deliberate Workflow

Pick a real task from your upcoming work. Design a multi-AI workflow using the patterns above. Execute it step by step, taking notes on:

1. How long each step takes
2. How well each AI performs its step
3. How smooth the handoffs are
4. What the final quality is compared to what you'd get from a single AI

Here's a starter task if you don't have one in mind:

Task: Write a recommendation memo for your team about which project management tool to adopt.

Workflow: 1. Perplexity: "Compare the top 5 project management tools for teams of 20–50 people in 2026. Include pricing, key features, user reviews, and notable limitations." 2. Claude: "Using this research [paste], write a 1,500-word recommendation memo. Evaluate the top three options against our requirements: [list your real requirements]. Recommend one with clear reasoning. The audience is my management team." 3. ChatGPT: "Create a comparison table as an image showing the top 3 tools with columns for: price per user, key features, integration options, user rating, and our recommendation." 4. Claude: "Review this memo for any gaps, unclear reasoning, or weak arguments. Suggest improvements."

Common Workflow Mistakes

Over-engineering. Not every task needs a five-step workflow. If you're writing a quick email, write it in one AI. Save multi-AI workflows for tasks where quality justifies the extra effort.

Too many handoffs. Each handoff is a chance for context loss. If you can combine two steps into one without losing quality, do it. Three steps is often the sweet spot — research, draft, polish.

Ignoring your own judgment. Multi-AI workflows work best with a human in the loop at each stage. Don't blindly pass output from one AI to the next. Review each step. Does the research look right? Does the draft capture what you wanted? Is the final product something you're proud of?

Inconsistent context. Telling one AI you're writing for executives and another that you're writing for junior staff produces incoherent output. Keep context consistent across the workflow.

The Bottom Line

Multi-AI workflows are the most advanced technique in this book, and they're what separates casual AI users from people who get extraordinary results. The concept is simple — chain the right AIs in the right order — but the impact is significant.

Start with the five patterns. Adapt them to your work. Practice the handoffs. And when someone asks how you consistently produce work that's well-researched, well-written, visually polished, and done faster than they'd expect — you'll know your secret.

It's not that you have better tools than everyone else. It's that you use them together.

Chapter 13: The Art of the Handoff

Chapter 12 introduced multi-AI workflows. This chapter goes deep on the trickiest part: moving context between AI assistants without losing the thread. The handoff is where most multi-AI workflows shine or fall apart. Get it right, and your output is seamless. Get it wrong, and you spend more time re-explaining context than you saved by using multiple tools.

Why Handoffs Are Hard

When you switch from one AI to another, you're starting from zero. The new AI has no memory of what you discussed with the old one. It doesn't know your project, your goals, your constraints, or the decisions you've already made.

This is fundamentally different from handing off work between humans, where shared organizational knowledge, previous meetings, and institutional memory provide background context. AI has none of that. Every conversation starts blank.

The quality of your handoff — the information you carry from one AI to the next — determines the quality of the result. A great handoff gives the new AI everything it needs to continue at the level the previous AI left off. A bad one makes the new AI start over, wasting the progress you've made.

The Handoff Template

Through extensive testing, I've developed a handoff template that works for most transitions. Here it is:

```
### Context
[What is this project? Who is the audience? What has been done so far?]

### Previous Work
[Summary of what the previous AI produced. Key findings, decisions, and outputs.]

### Key Decisions Already Made
[List any decisions or directions that shouldn't be revisited.]

### What I Need From You
[Specific task for this AI. What format, length, tone, and deliverables?]
```

```
### Constraints
[Any limitations, requirements, or things to avoid.]
```

Let me show you this in practice.

Example: Research-to-Writing Handoff

Bad handoff (what most people do):

Paste the entire Perplexity output into Claude and say: "Write an article about this."

What goes wrong: Claude doesn't know the audience, the tone, the length, which findings matter, or what the article's point is. It makes all these decisions itself, often poorly.

Good handoff:

Context

> I'm writing a 2,000-word article for our company blog about remote work trends in 2026. Our audience is HR professionals and team leaders. The tone should be professional but accessible — not academic.

Previous Work

> I researched this topic in Perplexity. Key findings: - 62% of companies now offer hybrid work, up from 47% in 2024 (source: Flex Index) - AI tools have reduced the "productivity gap" between remote and in-office workers to near zero (source: Stanford Remote Work Study) - The biggest remaining challenge is social connection and mentoring (source: multiple) - Companies that mandate full return-to-office are seeing 12% higher attrition (source: Revelio Labs)

Key Decisions Already Made

- The article argues FOR hybrid work, with honest acknowledgment of its challenges
- We want to cite all statistics with their sources
- We don't want to mention our own product (this is educational content, not marketing)

What I Need From You

Write the full 2,000-word article. Include an engaging introduction, clear sections with headers, and a forward-looking conclusion. Maintain the citations from the research.

Constraints

- No jargon that a non-HR person wouldn't understand
- Don't use phrases like "in today's rapidly evolving landscape" or "it's worth noting that"
- Include at least one specific example or case study (you can use a realistic but clearly hypothetical one if needed)

What goes right: Claude has everything it needs. The output will be on target from the first draft.

Handoff Types

Different types of transitions require different handoff approaches.

Research → Writing

This is the most common handoff. You've gathered information and now need it turned into prose.

What to carry over: - Key findings (summarized, not raw) - Sources and citations - Any specific data points that must be included - Gaps in the research (so the writer doesn't invent information to fill them)

What to add: - Audience and tone - Format and length - Point of view or argument - Structure preferences

Common mistake: Dumping the entire Perplexity output into Claude. Perplexity's output comes with its own framing, headers, and organization. Claude doesn't need that structure — it needs the information. Summarize the key findings in your own words and include the specific data points and citations.

Writing → Editing/Review

You have a draft and want a different AI to critique or edit it.

What to carry over: - The complete draft - The original brief (audience, purpose) - Any feedback you've already identified

What to add: - Specific aspects to review (tone? accuracy? structure? persuasiveness?) - Whether you want light editing or substantial critique - Any elements that are fixed and shouldn't be changed

Common mistake: Asking the new AI to "review this" without context. Without knowing the audience and purpose, it can't evaluate whether the draft achieves its goals. "Review this board memo for clarity and persuasiveness" is much better than "review this."

Brainstorming → Development

You've generated options in one AI and want to develop the best one in another.

What to carry over: - The full list of options generated - Which option you're choosing and why - The evaluation criteria used

What to add: - How you want the chosen option developed (in what detail, to what specification) - The format of the final output - Any elements from the rejected options that should be incorporated

Common mistake: Only carrying over the winning option. The context of what was considered and rejected helps the new AI understand the thinking behind the call.

Data Analysis → Narrative

You've analyzed data in one AI and need a narrative explanation in another.

What to carry over: - The key findings (in words, not just charts) - The methodology (what was analyzed and how) - Any surprising or counterintuitive findings - The actual numbers that matter

What to add: - The narrative context (why was this analysis done?) - The audience for the narrative - What decisions the narrative should inform

Common mistake: Carrying the charts but not the insights. Claude can't see ChatGPT's matplotlib charts unless you describe them or upload them as images. Translate the visual findings into words.

Context Compression

One of the most valuable skills for multi-AI work is context compression: taking a long, detailed interaction with one AI and distilling it into a tight handoff for the next.

The Summary Technique

Before switching AIs, ask the current AI to summarize the work done:

> "Summarize our conversation so far. Include: (1) the key decisions we made, (2) the main findings, (3) the current state of the work, and (4) what still needs to be done. Format it so I can give this summary to another AI assistant to continue the work."

That gives you a ready-made handoff document. The technique saves significant time and produces better continuity than trying to summarize the conversation yourself.

The Decision Log

For complex projects that span multiple AI sessions, maintain a running decision log:

```
Decision Log - [Project Name]
1. [Date] Decided to target HR professionals, not general audience
2. [Date] Chose hybrid-work angle over fully-remote angle
```

```
3. [Date] Key stat: 62% hybrid adoption rate (Flex Index)
4. [Date] Draft structure: 6 sections, ~2000 words
```

The log travels with you across AIs and ensures no important decision gets lost in the handoff.

Try This: The Compression Challenge

Take a long conversation you've had with an AI (at least 10 turns). Ask the AI to compress it into a handoff document using the template above. Then open a new conversation in a different AI, paste the handoff, and ask it to continue the work.

Compare the continuation with what would have happened if you'd started over from scratch in the new AI. The difference demonstrates the value of structured handoffs.

Cross-Platform Data Transfer

Beyond conversational context, you often need to move actual data between platforms.

Text

Simple: Copy-paste. Works for most text content. **Better**: For long text, save it as a file and upload it. Avoids copy-paste formatting issues and ensures nothing gets truncated. **Best**: For structured information, format it as markdown before transferring. Every AI assistant understands markdown.

Files

CSV/Excel: Download from ChatGPT's data analysis → upload to Claude or Gemini **Documents**: Most platforms accept PDF, DOCX, and TXT uploads **Images**: Download from ChatGPT's image generation → upload to Gemini or describe to Claude

Code

From ChatGPT: Copy code blocks directly **From Claude Code**: Code changes are made directly in your files, so there's nothing to transfer **From GitHub Copilot**: Code is already in your IDE

Limitations

- You can't share a conversation from one AI with another directly (no cross-platform "share link")
- Chat history doesn't transfer between platforms
- Custom instructions in one AI don't carry over to another
- Files uploaded to one AI aren't accessible to another

These limitations are why the handoff template matters. It's the bridge between siloed platforms.

When Not to Hand Off

Sometimes the best handoff is no handoff. Stay with one AI when:

You've built significant context. If you've spent twenty minutes giving Claude background on your project, don't switch to ChatGPT for a subtask Claude can handle adequately. The context you've built is valuable.

The task is small. Don't fire up Perplexity to fact-check one minor claim in a Claude conversation. Ask Claude. If it's uncertain, it'll say so, and then you can verify.

Consistency matters. If you're producing a series of documents that need a consistent tone and style, switching AIs mid-series creates jarring inconsistencies. Pick one and stick with it.

The overhead exceeds the benefit. A handoff takes time — writing the context, switching tools, re-establishing the work. If the task would take ten minutes in the current AI and eight in the "better" AI, the two minutes saved don't justify five minutes of handoff overhead.

Advanced Handoff Techniques

The Parallel Path

Instead of a linear workflow (AI 1 → AI 2 → AI 3), sometimes you can run steps in parallel:

- Research in Perplexity while simultaneously brainstorming structure in ChatGPT
- Generate images in ChatGPT while writing text in Claude
- Analyze data in ChatGPT while drafting the narrative framework in Claude

Parallel paths save time but require you to merge the outputs later — its own skill.

The Feedback Loop

Instead of a one-way handoff, create a loop:

1. Draft in Claude
2. Critique in ChatGPT
3. Revise in Claude based on critique
4. Final review in ChatGPT
5. Final polish in Claude

Each iteration improves the output. Diminishing returns kick in after 2–3 loops, but the first loop almost always produces a significant improvement.

The Specialist Consultation

For specific technical questions within a broader project:

1. You're writing a health article in Claude
2. You need to verify a medical claim → switch to Perplexity
3. Perplexity confirms/corrects the claim → switch back to Claude with the verified information
4. Continue writing in Claude

This is less a full handoff and more a quick consultation. Keep it lightweight — the specific question and answer, not a full context transfer.

Building Handoff Habits

Like any skill, good handoffs become second nature with practice. Here's how to build the habit:

1. **Week 1**: Use the handoff template for every cross-AI transition. It'll feel slow. That's fine.
2. **Week 2**: Start using the summary technique at the end of long conversations.
3. **Week 3**: Experiment with parallel paths and feedback loops.
4. **Week 4**: By now you'll have internalized the pattern and won't need the template. You'll include the right context in every transition naturally.

The Bottom Line

The handoff is the unsexy but critical skill that makes multi-AI workflows actually work. Research and writing and analysis are the glamorous parts. The handoff is the plumbing. But anyone who's lived through a plumbing failure knows the plumbing matters more than the fixtures.

Invest in handoff skills. Use the template. Compress context effectively. Know when to hand off and when to stay. The quality of your multi-AI work will be directly proportional to the quality of your handoffs.

Chapter 14: Managing Your AI Toolkit

AI subscriptions add up. Five platforms at $20/month each is $1,200/year. That's real money for most people and a line item most businesses have to justify. This chapter helps you optimize your spending, manage your accounts, and get the most capability for the least cost.

The Subscription Landscape (Mid-2026)

Here's the current pricing, so you can make informed decisions:

Free Tiers

Every major platform offers a free tier:

- **ChatGPT Free**: Access to GPT-5.5 mini with limited GPT-5.5 usage. Image generation with limits. Basic browsing.
- **Claude Free**: Access to Claude Sonnet with daily message limits. No Projects feature on free tier.
- **Gemini Free**: Access to Gemini models through Google. Basic integration with Workspace.
- **Copilot Free**: Basic Copilot features in Edge, Windows. Limited capabilities.
- **Perplexity Free**: Limited daily searches. Basic features.

The free tiers are genuinely useful. For occasional use, you may not need to pay anything. But the limits are real — you'll hit message caps during heavy use, and advanced features sit behind the paywall.

Paid Individual Tiers

Platform	Plan	Price	Key Additions
ChatGPT	Plus	$20/month	Full GPT-5.5 access, native image gen, Advanced Data Analysis, higher limits
Claude	Pro	$20/month	Higher limits, Opus 4.7 access, Projects, priority access

Platform	Plan	Price	Key Additions
Google AI	Pro	$19.99/month	Gemini 3 Pro, 1,000 AI credits, Gemini in Workspace
Google AI	Plus	$7.99/month	Lighter Gemini access (US, January 2026)
Copilot	Pro	$20/month	Priority GPT-5.5, Copilot in Office apps, image generation
Perplexity	Pro	$20/month	Unlimited Pro searches, file uploads, advanced models
GitHub Copilot	Individual	$10/month	AI code completion in IDE

Business/Team Tiers

Platform	Plan	Price	Key Additions
ChatGPT	Team	$25–30/user/month	Admin controls, shared workspace, no training on data
Claude	Team	$28–30/user/month	Team workspace, higher limits, admin controls
Microsoft 365 Copilot	Business	$18–21/user/month	Office integration for orgs up to 300 users
Microsoft 365 Copilot	Enterprise	$30/user/month	Full Office integration, enterprise security
Microsoft 365 E7	Frontier Suite	$99/user/month	Copilot + Agent 365 + Entra Suite + E5 (May 2026 launch)
Google AI	Ultra	$249.99/month	Gemini 3.1 Pro, Deep Think, Veo 3.1, 25,000 AI credits
Gemini	Workspace add-on	Included in Workspace plans with AI add-on	Full Workspace integration
GitHub Copilot	Business	$19/user/month	Organization management, policy controls
GitHub Copilot	Enterprise	$39/user/month	Custom models, audit log streaming

Choosing Your Subscriptions

The core question: which subscriptions should you actually pay for?

The One-Subscription Recommendation

If you can only pay for one, make it either **ChatGPT Plus** or **Claude Pro**. Both are $20/month, and the choice depends on what you do most:

- **ChatGPT Plus** if you do a lot of: data analysis, image generation, general-purpose tasks, browsing, or voice conversation
- **Claude Pro** if you do a lot of: writing, coding, document analysis, careful reasoning, or work requiring long context windows

Use the free tiers of everything else.

The Two-Subscription Sweet Spot

For most knowledge workers, two paid subscriptions plus free tiers cover 95% of needs:

Option A: ChatGPT Plus + Claude Pro ($40/month) The power combo. ChatGPT handles data, images, and breadth. Claude handles writing, coding, and depth. Use Perplexity's free tier for occasional research, Gemini's free tier when you're in Google's ecosystem.

Option B: Claude Pro + Perplexity Pro ($40/month) For research-heavy professionals (journalists, analysts, academics). Claude for writing and analysis, Perplexity for cited research. Use ChatGPT's free tier for occasional data analysis and image generation.

Option C: ChatGPT Plus + GitHub Copilot ($30/month) For developers. ChatGPT for general tasks and data analysis, GitHub Copilot for daily coding. Use Claude's free tier for code review and writing.

The Three-Subscription Pro Stack

ChatGPT Plus + Claude Pro + Perplexity Pro ($60/month) Covers all bases: research (Perplexity), writing and coding (Claude), data and images (ChatGPT). Use Gemini and Copilot free tiers for ecosystem integration tasks.

The Developer's Stack

Claude Pro + GitHub Copilot Individual ($30/month) Claude Code for agent-level coding, GitHub Copilot for inline completion. Add ChatGPT Plus ($20/month) if you also need data analysis and image generation.

The Ecosystem-First Approach

If you're deeply embedded in one ecosystem:

Google users: Gemini Advanced ($20/month) + one other (Claude Pro or ChatGPT Plus) **Microsoft users**: Copilot Pro ($20/month) + one other (Claude Pro or ChatGPT Plus)

The ecosystem tool handles your integrated tasks, and the other handles standalone quality.

Annual vs. Monthly Billing

Most platforms offer a discount for annual billing:

- ChatGPT Plus: $200/year (save $40 vs. monthly)
- Claude Pro: Some annual options may be available; check current pricing
- Perplexity Pro: $200/year (save $40 vs. monthly)
- GitHub Copilot: $100/year (save $20 vs. monthly)

My recommendation: Pay monthly for the first three months. That gives you time to see whether each tool is actually worth it. Once you're sure, switch to annual for the savings. Don't lock in a yearly subscription for a tool you might drop after the novelty wears off.

Cost Optimization Strategies

Strategy 1: The Rotation

Instead of maintaining three subscriptions simultaneously, rotate:

- Month 1: ChatGPT Plus + Claude Pro
- Month 2: Claude Pro + Perplexity Pro
- Month 3: ChatGPT Plus + Perplexity Pro

You get access to all three paid tiers for $40/month instead of $60/month, at the cost of never having all three available at once. Works well if your needs shift project-to-project.

Strategy 2: The Free Tier Max

Use free tiers as aggressively as possible:

- Start every task in the free tier of the appropriate platform
- Only use your paid subscription when you hit a limit or need a paid feature
- Reserve paid-tier usage for tasks where the quality difference justifies it

Strategy 3: The API Alternative

For heavy users with technical skills, API access can beat subscriptions on cost:

- OpenAI API: Pay per token (GPT-5.5 runs roughly $5–30 per million tokens depending on input/output and tier)
- Anthropic API: Pay per token (Sonnet 4.6 is roughly $3–15, Opus 4.7 roughly $15–75 per million tokens; cache hits are dramatically cheaper)
- Google API: Generous free tier, then pay per token (Gemini 3 Pro / 3.1 Pro roughly $2–12 per million tokens)
- DeepSeek API: Open-weight V4 Pro / V4 Flash at roughly 10× cheaper than premium Western providers (V4 Flash $0.14 input / $0.28 output per million tokens)

For someone sending 50 messages per day, the API might run $10–30/month versus $20/month for a subscription. But you lose the UI, file upload, and other consumer features. Mainly worth it for developers or people building AI into their workflows programmatically.

Strategy 4: Employer-Provided Access

Check whether your employer provides any AI subscriptions:

- Many companies now include Copilot in Microsoft 365 licensing
- Some provide GitHub Copilot for all developers
- A growing number offer ChatGPT Team or Claude Team access

If your employer provides one platform, you only need to pay for personal subscriptions to the others.

Account Management

Managing multiple AI accounts introduces practical challenges.

Password Management

Use a password manager (1Password, Bitwarden, Dashlane, etc.) for your AI accounts. You'll end up with at least five accounts across different platforms, each with different credentials.

Email Organization

Each platform sends different types of email: - Usage alerts - Feature announcements - Billing notifications - Newsletter content

Create an email filter or folder for AI platform mail so it stays out of your inbox without burying billing issues.

Data Organization

Your work is scattered across platforms: - ChatGPT conversation history - Claude conversation history - Perplexity search history - Generated images in ChatGPT - Documents uploaded to various platforms

Best practice: Don't rely on any AI platform as your document storage. Save important outputs — finished documents, generated images, key research findings — to your own storage (local drive, cloud storage). AI platforms change retention policies, suffer outages, and occasionally lose data.

Try This: The Account Audit

Open every AI platform you have an account with. For each one, check:

1. What plan are you on? (Free or paid?)
2. When does your billing cycle end?
3. What's your usage like? (How often do you actually use it?)
4. Are there features of the paid plan you're not using?
5. Is there a feature you wish you had access to?

This audit often surfaces surprises: a paid subscription you forgot about, a platform you barely use, or free-tier limits that never actually bothered you.

Data Portability

One under-discussed aspect of multi-AI use is data portability: can you get your data out of one platform and into another?

Conversation Export

- **ChatGPT**: Settings → Data Controls → Export Data. Gives you a ZIP file of all conversations in JSON format.
- **Claude**: Export functionality varies; check current settings for data export options.
- **Gemini**: Google Takeout includes Gemini conversation data.
- **Perplexity**: Limited export options for search history.

Content Portability

The content you create with AI (documents, code, analysis) is yours. Save it locally. The platforms don't claim ownership of your conversations or outputs (check current terms of service for specifics, but that's the general practice across all major platforms).

The Vendor Lock-In Question

"Will I get locked into one platform?" Many people worry about this. The short answer: not really. Here's why:

- AI conversations are inherently transient. You don't build up years of structured data in an AI assistant the way you do in a CRM or email system.
- The skills you develop are transferable. Learning to prompt well in one AI makes you better at prompting all of them.
- Custom assistants (GPTs, Claude Projects, Gems) take some investment, but they're relatively simple to recreate on another platform.

The biggest lock-in risk is ecosystem integration. If you've built workflows around Copilot in Office 365 or Gemini in Workspace, switching ecosystems is painful. But that's a Microsoft/Google lock-in issue, not an AI lock-in issue.

Tracking Your ROI

If you're spending money on AI subscriptions — especially expensing them or justifying them to a manager — track your ROI:

Simple Time-Savings Log

For two weeks, every time you use an AI assistant, estimate: - How long the task took with AI - How long it would have taken without AI - Which platform you used

At the end of two weeks, add up the time saved. Multiply by your hourly rate (or your employer's cost per hour for your role). Compare to subscription costs.

In my experience, even one paid AI subscription returns 10–50x its cost in time savings for active users. The math is rarely close.

Quality Improvements

Time isn't the only return. Track quality wins too: - Did the AI help you catch an error? - Was a document better-written because of AI assistance? - Did AI-assisted research surface information you wouldn't have found? - Did a presentation land better because of AI-generated visuals?

Quality improvements are harder to quantify but often more valuable than time savings.

The Future of AI Pricing

A brief note on where things are heading:

Prices will likely decrease. As competition intensifies and models grow more efficient, subscription prices may drop, or capabilities at each price point may rise. The $20/month price point has been remarkably stable, but what you get for $20/month has increased substantially.

Bundling is coming. Apple Intelligence ships with Apple devices. Google bundles Gemini with Workspace. Microsoft bundles Copilot with certain Microsoft 365 plans. Expect more bundling as AI becomes a standard feature rather than a premium add-on.

Usage-based pricing may expand. Some platforms may move toward (or add) pay-per-use pricing alongside subscriptions, particularly for resource-intensive features like image generation and long-context analysis.

Enterprise is the bigger market. Platform companies are increasingly focused on enterprise sales, where per-user pricing at scale generates serious revenue. Consumer pricing may grow more competitive as the enterprise market expands.

The Bottom Line

You don't need to spend $100/month on AI subscriptions. Two subscriptions ($40/month) cover the vast majority of use cases. One subscription plus free tiers ($20/month) covers most needs for lighter users.

Match your subscriptions to your actual usage, not to what sounds impressive. The best AI toolkit is the one you actually use, not the one with the most subscriptions.

Audit your accounts quarterly. Drop what you don't use. Add what you need. And save your important work locally — no platform should be your only copy of anything that matters.

Part IV: Cross-Platform Strategies

"Strategy without tactics is the slowest route to victory. Tactics without strategy is the noise before defeat."

— Sun Tzu (attributed)

Chapter 15: Privacy and Data Across Platforms

When you type a prompt into an AI assistant, where does that text go? Who can read it? Does it get used to train the next version of the model? If you upload a confidential contract, does the AI company now have access to your trade secrets?

These questions matter. And the answers differ for every platform.

This chapter gives you the straight facts about what each major AI platform does with your data, how to protect your privacy, and how to make informed decisions about what to share with which AI.

The Core Privacy Questions

For every AI platform, you need answers to four questions:

1. **Is my data used to train the model?** If yes, your conversations could shape future model behavior, and in theory, fragments of your input could surface in outputs to other users. (In practice, that's rare, but the risk exists.)
2. **Who at the company can see my conversations?** Human reviewers at AI companies sometimes read conversations for quality assurance and safety monitoring.
3. **How long is my data retained?** Some platforms keep your conversations forever. Others delete them after a period. Some let you delete them yourself.
4. **What happens if there's a data breach?** Your conversation history with an AI may contain sensitive personal, business, or financial information. What protections exist?

Platform-by-Platform Privacy Breakdown

ChatGPT (OpenAI)

Training data usage: - **Free and Plus plans**: Opt-in by default. Your conversations may be used to train future models unless you opt out in Settings → Data Controls → "Improve the model for everyone." When you opt out, your conversations are still retained for safety monitoring but aren't used for training. - **Team and Enterprise plans**: Conversations are NOT used for training. This is one of the main reasons businesses pay for higher-tier plans.

Human review: - OpenAI employees may review conversations for safety and quality, regardless of your training opt-out setting. Opted-out conversations are reviewed less frequently.

Data retention: - Conversations are retained in your account history until you delete them. You can delete individual conversations or your entire history. - Even after deletion from your account, OpenAI may retain data for up to 30 days for safety purposes. - Enterprise plans have configurable retention policies.

Key privacy features: - Temporary Chat mode: Conversations aren't saved to history or used for training. - Data export: You can download all your conversation data. - Conversation deletion: Available at individual and bulk levels.

The honest assessment: On the free and Plus plans with default settings, assume OpenAI can see and use your conversations. Opt out of training if you care about privacy. Don't share genuinely sensitive information — trade secrets, personal financial data, health records — unless you're on an Enterprise plan with appropriate agreements.

Claude (Anthropic)

Training data usage: - **Free, Pro, and Max plans**: Opt-in by default since Anthropic's August 28, 2025 consumer-terms update. Conversations and coding sessions can be used to improve future Claude models unless you opt out in Privacy Settings. Opting in extends data retention to up to five years; opting out keeps the standard 30-day window. - **Team, Enterprise, API, Claude for Work, Claude for Government, and Claude for Education**: Excluded from model training by default under the Commercial Terms. Stronger contractual guarantees.

Human review: - Anthropic may review conversations flagged by automated safety systems. Their policy is to minimize human review of user conversations.

Data retention: - Conversations are retained in your account until deleted. You can delete individual conversations. - Opt-out (default for new users who don't change the setting): 30 days. - Opt-in: up to five years. - You can change your training preference at any time in Privacy Settings.

Key privacy features: - Explicit, in-app choice on training participation (existing users were prompted in September 2025) - Enterprise data isolation - SOC 2 Type II compliance

The honest assessment: Anthropic's August 2025 policy change brought its consumer defaults in line with OpenAI's. Free, Pro, and Max users should make a deliberate choice in Privacy Settings rather than accept the default opt-in. The genuine privacy advantage now lives at the Team, Enterprise, and API tiers (training-excluded by default) — the same place it lives for OpenAI. For sensitive work, the tier matters more than the brand.

Gemini (Google)

Training data usage: - **Free tier**: Conversations may be used to improve Google products, including Gemini. Human reviewers may read conversations. - **Google One AI Premium / Workspace**: Different data handling. Workspace conversations are covered by Google Workspace's data processing terms, which generally don't use content for training.

Human review: - Google explicitly states that human reviewers may read Gemini conversations, using them for quality, safety, and product improvement.

Data retention: - Gemini conversations are retained and linked to your Google account. - You can delete conversation history through your Google account's My Activity page. - Retention period: Up to 18 months for review conversations (or until you delete them).

Key privacy features: - My Activity controls for deletion - Workspace data processing agreements for business users - Data regionalization options for Workspace

The honest assessment: Google collects a lot of data across all its products, and Gemini is no exception. Treat free-tier Gemini conversations as Google data

— which means Google can read and use them. Workspace users have stronger protections. If privacy is your primary concern, free-tier Gemini is the weakest option among the major platforms.

Copilot (Microsoft)

Training data usage: - **Free Copilot**: Conversations may be used to improve Microsoft products. - **Copilot Pro**: Similar to free, with somewhat stronger data handling. - **Microsoft 365 Copilot (Business)**: Data is processed under Microsoft's commercial data protection terms. Conversations are NOT used for training. Data stays within your organization's Microsoft 365 boundary.

Human review: - Microsoft may review conversations for safety and quality on consumer plans. - Business and Enterprise plans have strict data processing agreements that limit human review.

Data retention: - Consumer: Retained in your Microsoft account. - Business: Governed by your organization's Microsoft 365 retention policies.

Key privacy features: - Commercial data protection for business plans - Compliance with GDPR, HIPAA, and other regulations (on enterprise plans) - Data stays within your Microsoft 365 tenant (business)

The honest assessment: Microsoft 365 Copilot for business is one of the strongest options for privacy because it runs inside the same data protection framework enterprises already trust for email and documents. Consumer Copilot has weaker protections. The gap between consumer and business Copilot on privacy is the largest of any platform.

Perplexity

Training data usage: - Perplexity's privacy policy states that they may use interaction data to improve their products. - The nature of Perplexity's product (search) means your queries are sent to external search engines and web sources.

Human review: - Less publicly documented than other platforms. Assume some review is possible.

Data retention: - Search history is retained in your account. - You can delete search history.

Key privacy features: - Search history deletion - Enterprise tiers with stronger data protections

The honest assessment: Perplexity is unique because your queries go to external search engines, which exposes your questions to third parties beyond Perplexity itself. For sensitive topics, know that your Perplexity searches may be visible to search engine providers.

The Privacy Decision Framework

How to decide what to share with which AI:

Tier 1: Share Freely

Information that's public or not sensitive: - General knowledge questions - Public document analysis - Creative brainstorming - Learning and education

Any platform is fine.

Tier 2: Share with Caution

Information that's professional but not classified: - Business writing (without confidential specifics) - Code from open-source or non-proprietary projects - General business analysis

Opt out of training on whichever consumer plan you use, or use your employer-provided enterprise platform.

Tier 3: Share Only on Enterprise Plans

Information that's confidential: - Client data - Proprietary business strategies - Financial details - Legal documents - Customer information

Use only enterprise/business plans with data processing agreements: Microsoft 365 Copilot, Claude Enterprise, ChatGPT Enterprise.

Tier 4: Don't Share with Any AI

Information that's highly sensitive: - Passwords and credentials - Social Security numbers, credit card numbers - Medical records (unless using a HIPAA-compliant setup) - Information covered by NDA that specifically prohibits AI processing - Classified government information

Keep this out of AI assistants entirely.

Practical Privacy Strategies

Strategy 1: Anonymize Before You Ask

Before pasting sensitive information into an AI, strip identifying details:

- Replace company names with "Company A," "Company B"
- Replace people's names with "Person 1," "Person 2"
- Replace specific financial figures with ranges or relative terms
- Remove dates that could identify specific events

You get the AI's analytical capabilities without exposing the actual sensitive details.

Strategy 2: Use the Right Platform for the Sensitivity Level

Build a habit of weighing sensitivity before choosing your platform:

- Casual task? Use whatever's convenient.
- Professional task? Make sure you've opted out of training on your chosen consumer plan, or use your organization's enterprise tool.
- Sensitive task? Enterprise platform only.
- Highly sensitive? Don't use AI, or use a local model (Ollama + Llama).

Strategy 3: Run Local Models for Maximum Privacy

For truly sensitive work, run AI models on your own hardware:

- **Ollama** lets you run open-source models (Llama, Mistral, etc.) locally
- Data never leaves your machine
- Quality is lower than cloud models, but privacy is absolute
- Requires decent hardware (16GB+ RAM, preferably with a GPU)

The nuclear option: maximum privacy, minimum convenience. For some use cases, it's the right call.

Strategy 4: Compartmentalize

Don't mix personal and professional AI use on the same account:

- Use your personal email for personal AI accounts
- Use your work email for work AI accounts
- Use different browsers or profiles to keep them separate

That keeps personal conversations from bleeding into professional ones, and vice versa.

Try This: The Privacy Audit

For each AI platform you use, answer these questions:

1. What plan am I on? (Free, Pro, Enterprise?)
2. Have I opted out of training data usage where possible?
3. What's the most sensitive thing I've put into this platform?
4. Was that an appropriate thing to share given the platform's privacy policy?
5. Would I be comfortable if my conversations on this platform were made public?

If question 5 makes you uncomfortable, either change your behavior or upgrade to a more privacy-protective plan.

The Regulatory Landscape

Privacy regulations affect what you can and should do with AI:

GDPR (EU): Affects anyone processing data of EU residents. Most AI platforms comply with GDPR, but be aware of data-transfer implications (your data may be processed in the US).

CCPA/CPRA (California): Gives California residents rights over their personal data, including data used in AI conversations.

Industry-specific regulations: HIPAA (healthcare), FERPA (education), SOX (financial), and others may restrict what data you can put into AI systems. If you work in a regulated industry, check with compliance before using AI with any sensitive data.

Company policies: Your employer may have specific AI use policies. A growing number of organizations have written rules about which AI platforms are approved and what data can be shared. Follow them.

What Each Platform Knows About You

Beyond your conversations, AI platforms collect other data:

- **Usage patterns**: When you use the platform, how often, what features you use
- **Device information**: Browser, operating system, IP address, location
- **Account information**: Email, name, payment details
- **Interaction data**: Response ratings, regeneration patterns, feature usage

This metadata feeds product improvement, personalization, and business analytics. It's separate from conversation content but still counts as personal data under most privacy regulations.

The Privacy-Quality Trade-Off

There's an inherent tension between privacy and AI quality:

- AI companies improve their models using real conversation data
- More data → better models → better results for you
- But sharing your data means giving up privacy

Where you land on this spectrum is a personal decision. Some people are happy to share conversations to help improve AI (and benefit from the improvements). Others want maximum privacy regardless of the cost to model improvement.

Neither position is wrong. But make an informed choice rather than accepting defaults.

The Bottom Line

AI privacy is a spectrum, not a binary. The right approach depends on what you're doing:

- **Casual use**: Default settings on any platform are fine
- **Professional use**: Opt out of training on whichever consumer plan you use, or use enterprise plans on any platform
- **Sensitive data**: Enterprise plans only, or local models
- **Highly sensitive data**: Don't use cloud AI

The most important habit: pause before you paste. Take one second to ask, "Is this appropriate to share with this platform at this privacy level?" That one-second habit prevents most privacy mistakes.

No AI insight is worth a data breach, a compliance violation, or a broken NDA. Use AI aggressively, but use it wisely.

Chapter 16: Prompt Portability

You've crafted the perfect prompt. It works beautifully in ChatGPT. You get exactly the output you want, every time. Then you paste that same prompt into Claude and get something completely different. Not bad, necessarily — just different. Different structure, different tone, different interpretation of your instructions.

This happens all the time, and it's one of the more frustrating aspects of working across multiple AI platforms. This chapter explains why prompts don't transfer cleanly between AIs and shows you how to adapt your approach for each platform.

Why the Same Prompt Gets Different Results

Three factors drive prompt variability across platforms:

1. Different Training Data and RLHF

Each model was trained on different data and fine-tuned with different human feedback. They've learned different interpretations of ambiguous instructions. When you say "write a professional email," each model has a slightly different understanding of what "professional" means, how long the email should be, and what structure to use.

2. Different System Prompts

Every AI assistant has a system prompt — hidden instructions that shape its behavior before you say anything. ChatGPT's emphasizes helpfulness and breadth. Claude's emphasizes thoughtfulness and honesty. Gemini's emphasizes conciseness. These system prompts color every response to every user prompt.

3. Different Default Behaviors

Each AI has different defaults for things like: - Response length (Gemini defaults shorter, Claude defaults medium, ChatGPT defaults longer) - Formatting (ChatGPT loves bullet points, Claude uses more prose, Gemini varies) - Tone (ChatGPT is enthusiastic, Claude is measured, Gemini is direct) - Hedging (Claude hedges more, ChatGPT hedges less, Gemini varies)

What Transfers Well

Some prompting techniques work identically across all major platforms:

Role Assignment

"You are an experienced marketing consultant" works everywhere. All major AIs respond to role assignment, and the effect is similar: the response takes on the perspective and knowledge level of the assigned role.

Clear Formatting Instructions

"Respond in a numbered list," "use markdown headers," "format as a table with columns for X, Y, and Z" — formatting instructions transfer cleanly. All major AIs understand markdown and common formatting conventions.

Explicit Constraints

"Keep your response under 200 words," "do not use bullet points," "respond in Spanish" — hard constraints transfer well. The AIs may comply with varying degrees of strictness (Claude tends to be more obedient about word counts, ChatGPT sometimes goes over), but the intent comes through.

Step-by-Step Instructions

"First, analyze the data. Second, identify the top three trends. Third, write a summary of each trend." Numbered step-by-step instructions work across all platforms.

Examples (Few-Shot Prompting)

Providing examples of the desired output works universally and is one of the most powerful prompting techniques. "Here's an example of what I want: [example]. Now do the same for [new topic]." This works on every platform.

What Doesn't Transfer Well

Tone Descriptions

"Write in a casual, friendly tone" means different things to different AIs:

- **ChatGPT**: Casual + friendly = enthusiastic, peppy, lots of exclamation points, maybe an emoji
- **Claude**: Casual + friendly = conversational, warm, relaxed but still thoughtful
- **Gemini**: Casual + friendly = brief, accessible, informal

If tone matters, don't just describe it. Provide a sample paragraph in the desired tone and say "match this tone." That transfers far more reliably than adjective descriptions.

Length Expectations

"Write a detailed response" produces wildly different output lengths:

- **ChatGPT**: 800–1,500 words
- **Claude**: 500–1,000 words (Claude often defaults shorter unless asked for more)
- **Gemini**: 300–600 words

If length matters, specify it: "Write approximately 1,000 words" or "write 5–7 paragraphs." Don't leave it to the AI's read of "detailed."

Assumed Context

ChatGPT assumes you want a helpful, comprehensive answer. Claude assumes you want a thoughtful, accurate answer. Gemini assumes you want a concise, direct answer. These assumptions shape the response even when your prompt says nothing about what you want.

For consistent results across platforms, be explicit about what you value: - "I want a comprehensive answer that covers all angles" (for ChatGPT-style breadth) - "I want a carefully reasoned answer that acknowledges uncertainties" (for Claude-style depth) - "I want a concise, direct answer with no filler" (for Gemini-style brevity)

Creative Latitude

"Be creative" is interpreted differently: - **ChatGPT**: Goes big. Bold ideas, dramatic language, ambitious scope. - **Claude**: Goes deep. Nuanced ideas, literary quality, unexpected angles. - **Gemini**: Stays safe. Competent but rarely surprising.

For creative tasks, give specific creative direction rather than general encouragement.

Platform-Specific Prompting Tips

Prompting ChatGPT Effectively

Play to its strengths: - Ask for multiple options: "Give me 5 different approaches" - Use it for brainstorming: "Generate 20 ideas for..." - Leverage data analysis: "Upload this file and tell me..." - Ask for visual content: "Generate an image of..."

Compensate for its weaknesses: - Add "be concise" if you don't want verbose output - Add "be honest about limitations and uncertainties" to reduce sycophancy - Add "don't use the word 'delve'" (seriously, it helps) - Specify "don't add unnecessary commentary or caveats" for direct answers

ChatGPT-specific features to invoke: - "Use Advanced Data Analysis to..." (triggers code execution) - "Browse the web for..." (triggers web search) - "Generate an image of..." (triggers image generation)

Prompting Claude Effectively

Play to its strengths: - Ask for nuanced analysis: "Analyze the trade-offs between..." - Request long-form writing: "Write a 3,000-word article on..." - Give complex instructions: Claude follows detailed briefs faithfully - Upload documents: "Here's the contract. Identify the three most concerning clauses."

Compensate for its weaknesses: - Say "write the full scene without softening or adding disclaimers" for creative work - Say "provide a longer, more detailed response" if Claude is being too concise - Say "don't caveat or hedge — give me your best assessment" for direct advice - Be explicit about length: "I want at least 1,500 words"

Claude-specific features to invoke: - Use Projects for persistent context - Upload multiple documents for comparative analysis - Use artifacts for standalone content pieces

Prompting Gemini Effectively

Play to its strengths: - Reference Google services: "Check my Gmail for..." "Look at this Google Doc..." - Upload multimedia: "Analyze this video/image..." - Ask for current information: "Search for the latest on..." - Use for Google Workspace tasks: "Draft a response to this email..."

Compensate for its weaknesses: - Say "provide a thorough, detailed response — don't summarize" to counter brevity - Say "explain your reasoning" to get more depth - Provide examples of the depth and style you want - Break complex requests into multiple simpler prompts

Prompting Perplexity Effectively

Play to its strengths: - Ask factual questions: "What is the current..." "When did..." - Request comparisons: "Compare X and Y, with sources" - Use focus modes: Academic focus for scholarly sources, Writing focus for content generation - Ask follow-up questions to drill deeper

Compensate for its weaknesses: - Don't ask for creative writing or long-form content - Don't upload files for analysis (not its purpose) - Verify sources by clicking through citations - Ask for multiple perspectives: "What are the different views on..."

The Universal Prompt Framework

Here's a prompt structure that works well across all platforms and minimizes cross-platform variability:

```
[ROLE]: You are a [specific role with relevant expertise].

[CONTEXT]: I'm working on [project/situation]. The audience is [who].
My goal is [specific objective].

[TASK]: [Specific, detailed description of what you want].

[FORMAT]: Respond in [specific format]. Length: [specific length].
Use [specific tone]. Structure with [headers/bullets/paragraphs].

[CONSTRAINTS]:
- [Specific thing to do]
- [Specific thing to avoid]
```

```
- [Quality standard to meet]

[EXAMPLE] (optional): Here's an example of what good output looks like:
[paste example]
```

The framework works because it eliminates ambiguity. The more explicit you are, the less the AI's defaults matter, and the more consistent your results across platforms.

Try This: The Cross-Platform Prompt Test

Take a prompt you use frequently. Run it through the Universal Prompt Framework. Then test it on three AI platforms.

Compare: 1. How similar are the outputs? (If you used the framework, they should be more similar than with a vague prompt.) 2. Where do they still differ? (These gaps reveal the AI's persistent biases.) 3. Which platform handled it best? (That tells you where to use this prompt going forward.)

Building a Prompt Library

If you regularly work across multiple AIs, build a prompt library: a collection of tested, platform-adapted prompts for your common tasks.

Structure

```
Task: [What this prompt does]
Platform: [Which AI this version is for]
Prompt: [The actual prompt]
Notes: [Any tips or known issues]
Last tested: [Date]
```

Example Entry

```
Task: Generate weekly status report
Platform: Claude
Prompt: "You are a concise business writer. Using the following bullet points
of this week's accomplishments and blockers, write a professional status
report for my manager. Use headers for Accomplishments, Blockers, and
Next Week. Keep it under 400 words. Tone: professional but not stiff.
[paste bullet points]"
Notes: Claude handles this well; add "be thorough" if output is too brief
Last tested: March 2026
```

Platform-specific versions of your most-used prompts eliminate the "this prompt doesn't work in this AI" problem.

Side-by-Side: The Same Prompt, Three Different Results

The differences above are easier to understand when you see them in action. Here are real examples of identical prompts sent to ChatGPT, Claude, and Gemini, with the actual behavior you can expect from each.

Example 1: "Explain blockchain to a 10-year-old."

ChatGPT responds with enthusiasm and metaphor. It typically opens with something like "Imagine you and your friends have a special notebook..." and builds an extended analogy involving stickers, sharing, and everyone having a copy. The explanation runs 200–300 words, uses exclamation points, and ends with an encouraging line like "Pretty cool, right?"

Claude takes a more measured approach. It opens conversationally — "Think about how you keep track of who owes who in a group of friends" — and walks through the concept step by step. It's shorter, around 150–200 words, drops the excitement, and sticks to clarity. It might acknowledge what's hard to understand: "The tricky part is..."

Gemini is the most concise. It gives you a tight 80–120 word explanation, often structured as a few short paragraphs or a mini-list. The analogy is simpler and the language plainer, but it can feel less engaging to read aloud to a ten-year-old.

The takeaway: Same prompt, three different interpretations of what a ten-year-old needs. If you want engagement, ChatGPT. If you want clarity, Claude. If you want brevity, Gemini.

Example 2: "Write a professional email declining a meeting request."

ChatGPT produces a complete email with subject line, greeting, body, and sign-off. The tone is polite and slightly formal. It tends to offer alternatives ("I'd be happy to review any materials you can share via email") and runs about 120–150 words. It often slips in a line of encouragement you didn't ask for: "I appreciate you thinking of me!"

Claude also produces a full email, but the tone is warmer and more direct. It declines clearly in the first sentence rather than burying the "no" behind pleasantries. It's typically 80–120 words and reads like something you'd actually send without editing. It doesn't over-apologize.

Gemini gives the shortest version — often 60–80 words. The decline is efficient and professional, but it can feel abrupt. If you prefer directness, it's perfect. If your workplace culture values warmth, you'll need to add a sentence or two.

The takeaway: For emails, the "right" AI depends on your workplace culture. Formal environments suit ChatGPT's style. Straightforward teams prefer Claude. Fast-moving environments that prize brevity work well with Gemini.

Example 3: "List the pros and cons of remote work."

ChatGPT produces a detailed, balanced list — typically 5–7 items per side, each with a sentence or two of explanation. It formats with bold headers and sometimes adds a summary paragraph. Total output: 400–600 words.

Claude produces a similar list but with more nuance per item. Instead of just "Pro: flexible schedule," Claude might write "Pro: schedule flexibility — though this cuts both ways, since the freedom to work anytime can blur into the expectation that you're always available." It tends to acknowledge complexity. Total output: 300–500 words.

Gemini gives a clean, scannable list — typically 4–5 items per side with one sentence each. No elaboration, no nuance, just the facts. Total output: 150–250 words. Useful as a quick reference, but not enough if you're building an argument.

The takeaway: If you need the same prompt to produce comparable depth across platforms, you have to specify it. Adding "provide 5 items per side with 2–3 sentences of explanation each" would bring all three outputs much closer together. Without that specificity, each AI's defaults take over.

The Convergence Trend

One hopeful note: the major AIs are converging in their prompt understanding. Techniques that once worked only on one platform increasingly work on all of them. The gap between "what works on ChatGPT" and "what works on Claude" is smaller in early 2026 than it was in 2024.

As models improve, prompt portability is getting easier. But it's not there yet, and the nuances still matter for professional-quality output.

The Bottom Line

Prompts aren't perfectly portable between AI platforms. But you can minimize variability by:

1. Being explicit about everything: format, length, tone, style, constraints
2. Providing examples of desired output
3. Understanding each platform's defaults and compensating for them
4. Building platform-specific versions of your most-used prompts

The Universal Prompt Framework gets you 80% of the way to consistent results across platforms. Platform-specific adaptations get you the rest.

Think of it like driving different cars. The steering wheel and pedals work the same way, but each one has its quirks. Once you know the quirks, switching between them is effortless.

Chapter 17: Custom Assistants Across Platforms

Every major AI platform now lets you create custom assistants — specialized versions of the AI pre-configured for specific tasks, loaded with specific knowledge, and tuned for specific behaviors. It's one of the most powerful features in the AI landscape, and one of the most underused.

This chapter compares custom assistant capabilities across platforms and shows you how to build assistants that actually save time.

What Custom Assistants Do

At their core, custom assistants solve the "context reloading" problem. Instead of starting every conversation by explaining who you are, what you're working on, and how you want the AI to respond, a custom assistant comes pre-loaded with that context.

Think of the difference between calling a generic customer service line and calling someone who already knows your account, your history, and your preferences. The second conversation is faster, more relevant, and more productive.

Platform Comparison

ChatGPT: GPTs

OpenAI's custom assistant platform, available to ChatGPT Plus subscribers.

How they work: - You create a GPT through the GPT Builder interface - You provide a name, description, instructions, and optional knowledge files - The GPT can use ChatGPT's capabilities: web browsing, code execution, DALL-E, and third-party Actions (API integrations) - You can keep GPTs private, share them via link, or publish them to the GPT Store

Strengths: - Largest ecosystem. The GPT Store has thousands of community-created GPTs. Many are mediocre, but some are genuinely useful. - **Actions.** GPTs can connect to external APIs, letting them query databases, submit forms, or interact with third-party services. This is the most extensible custom assistant platform. - **File knowledge.** Upload documents (PDFs, text files, spreadsheets) as the GPT's knowledge base. It will reference them when responding. - **Easy creation.** The GPT Builder lets you create a GPT through conversation — you describe what you want, and it configures the GPT for you. - **Sharing.** Send a link to share your GPT with colleagues or the public.

Weaknesses: - **Knowledge retrieval quality.** GPTs sometimes fail to find relevant information in uploaded files, especially large ones. Retrieval isn't always reliable. - **Context window limits still apply.** A GPT with a lot of uploaded knowledge doesn't magically have unlimited context. It retrieves relevant chunks, which can miss important information. - **Store quality control.** The GPT Store is flooded with low-quality GPTs. Finding good ones takes trial and error. - **Instruction adherence.** GPTs sometimes drift from their instructions during long conversations.

Best GPTs to create: - A writing assistant with your company's style guide uploaded - A research assistant with your industry's key documents - A meeting prep assistant with your project documentation - A code review assistant with your coding standards

Claude: Projects

Anthropic's approach to persistent context, available to Claude Pro subscribers.

How they work: - You create a Project and add instructions and knowledge files - Every conversation within the Project has access to the Project's context - The Project instructions shape Claude's behavior for all conversations in that Project - Multiple conversations can exist within the same Project

Strengths: - **Context quality.** Claude Projects use the full context window effectively. Uploaded knowledge sits alongside your conversation rather than being retrieved in chunks. For documents up to the context window limit, Claude has access to the complete text. - **Instruction adherence.** Claude follows Project instructions more faithfully than GPTs follow theirs, in my testing. It drifts less over long conversations. - **Writing quality carries through.** Claude's writing strength applies within Projects. A writing assistant built as a Claude Project produces better prose than a comparable GPT. - **Simple and focused.** The Project interface is clean. No app store, no Actions, no plugins — just context and instructions. The simplicity is a feature.

Weaknesses: - **No external integrations.** Claude Projects can't connect to APIs or external services. It's a closed system: context in, conversation out. - **No sharing.** You can't easily share a Claude Project the way you can share a GPT link. - **Fewer knowledge file types.** The range of uploadable file types is narrower than GPTs. - **No code execution.** The Project can't run code. For data analysis inside a custom assistant, ChatGPT's GPTs are better.

Best Projects to create: - A writing assistant for a specific long-term writing project (upload all your research, style notes, and existing drafts) - A code assistant for a specific codebase (upload the architecture docs and coding standards) - A domain expert for your field (upload key reference materials) - A strategic advisor for your business (upload your business plan, market research, and competitive analysis)

Gemini: Gems

Google's custom assistant feature.

How they work: - You create a Gem with custom instructions - Gems can access Google services (if configured) - Available to Gemini Advanced subscribers

Strengths: - **Google ecosystem access.** A Gem can reference information from your Google Workspace, giving it unique access to your email, documents, and calendar. - **Quick creation.** Creating a Gem is straightforward and fast. - **Integration.** Gems work inside the Gemini interface alongside other Gemini features.

Weaknesses: - **Less mature.** Gems are newer and less feature-rich than GPTs or Claude Projects. - **Smaller ecosystem.** No equivalent of the GPT Store. - **Limited knowledge uploads.** The ability to upload custom knowledge is narrower than GPTs or Projects.

Best Gems to create: - A Workspace assistant that helps you manage Gmail, Docs, and Calendar tasks - A quick-reference assistant for frequently asked questions in your domain - A meeting assistant that integrates with Google Calendar and Meet

Copilot: Copilot Agents / Custom Copilots

Microsoft's custom assistant capabilities.

How they work: - Through Copilot Studio (for business users), you can create custom Copilots - These can integrate with Microsoft 365 data sources, Power Platform, and external systems - Consumer-level customization is more limited

Strengths: - **Enterprise integration.** Custom Copilots can access SharePoint, Dynamics 365, Teams, and other Microsoft business systems. For enterprise use cases, this is unmatched. - **Power Platform connection.** Custom Copilots can trigger Power Automate flows, query Dataverse, and integrate with business logic. - **Enterprise governance.** Admin controls, compliance features, and audit logging.

Weaknesses: - **Complexity.** Building a custom Copilot in Copilot Studio is far more involved than building a GPT or Claude Project. It's a developer/IT tool, not an end-user tool. - **Cost.** Enterprise Copilot features require additional licensing. - **Consumer gap.** Individual users don't have access to the powerful customization features available to business users.

Best Custom Copilots to create (for enterprise): - An HR assistant that answers employee questions from your company's policy documents - A sales assistant that pulls from CRM data - An IT help desk bot that resolves common issues - A project status assistant that aggregates data from multiple Microsoft 365 sources

Building Effective Custom Assistants

Regardless of platform, a few principles make custom assistants more effective:

Principle 1: Specific Instructions Beat Generic Ones

Bad: "You are a helpful writing assistant."

Good: "You are a writing assistant for Acme Corp's marketing team. You write in a professional but approachable tone. You use active voice. You never use jargon without defining it. Blog posts should be 800–1,200 words with a compelling headline, an introduction that hooks the reader, 3–5 substantive sections with headers, and a clear call to action. Use the brand voice guidelines in the uploaded documents."

The more specific your instructions, the more consistent and useful the assistant becomes.

Principle 2: Upload the Right Knowledge

Don't upload everything. Upload the specific documents the assistant actually needs:

- **For a writing assistant**: Style guide, brand voice document, examples of good writing
- **For a research assistant**: Key reference documents, data standards, methodology guidelines
- **For a domain expert**: Core reference materials, glossaries, recent publications
- **For a code assistant**: Architecture documentation, coding standards, API documentation

Too much uploaded knowledge can actually hurt performance, because the AI has to search through more material to find what's relevant.

Principle 3: Include Examples

The most effective custom-assistant instructions include examples of desired output:

> "When asked to draft a blog post, produce output like this example:
>
> [paste a real example of a good blog post in your style]
>
> Note the tone, structure, and use of subheadings. Match these patterns."

Examples are worth a thousand words of instruction.

Principle 4: Include Anti-Examples

Tell the assistant what NOT to do:

> "Do not: - Use passive voice unless specifically appropriate - Start paragraphs with 'Furthermore' or 'Moreover' - Include a conclusion that simply restates the introduction - Use buzzwords like 'synergy,' 'leverage,' or 'paradigm shift' - Add emoji or exclamation points unless the content is genuinely exciting"

Anti-examples prevent the most common failure modes.

Principle 5: Test and Iterate

Build the assistant, test it with real tasks, note what works and what doesn't, then refine the instructions. Good custom assistants usually take 3–5 iterations to get right.

Try This: Build Your First Custom Assistant

Pick your most common AI task. Build a custom assistant for it on your primary platform:

1. Write specific instructions covering the task, audience, tone, format, and constraints
2. Upload any relevant reference documents
3. Include at least one example of good output
4. Test it with five real tasks
5. Refine the instructions based on what worked and what didn't

Track how much time this saves over the next two weeks compared to starting from scratch each time.

Cross-Platform Custom Assistant Strategy

The optimal strategy uses custom assistants on multiple platforms, each suited to that platform's strengths:

The Recommended Setup

Claude Project: Your primary writing and analysis assistant. Upload your style guide, key reference documents, and project materials. Use this for all substantial writing and analytical work.

ChatGPT GPT: Your data and visual assistant. Configure it for your most common data analysis and image generation tasks. Include instructions about your preferred chart styles, brand colors, and reporting formats.

Gemini Gem (if you use Google Workspace): Your Workspace productivity assistant. Configure it for your email, calendar, and document management patterns.

Copilot (if you use Microsoft 365): Your Office productivity assistant, either using built-in Copilot or a custom Copilot through Copilot Studio.

Keeping Them in Sync

When you update your style guide, brand standards, or key reference materials, update them across all your custom assistants. That's the maintenance cost of a multi-platform setup, and it's worth flagging: every change has to propagate to each platform.

A practical approach: keep your master reference documents in one location (Google Drive, OneDrive, or a local folder) and re-upload when they change. Set a quarterly reminder to review and update all custom assistants.

The Bottom Line

Custom assistants are the difference between "using AI" and "having AI work for you." The upfront investment of building them (30–60 minutes per assistant) pays off within a few days through faster, more consistent, higher-quality output.

Build at least one custom assistant on your primary platform this week. You'll wonder how you ever worked without it.

Match each assistant's platform to the task: - Writing and analysis → Claude Project - Data and images → ChatGPT GPT - Workspace integration → Gemini Gem or Copilot

And remember: the best custom assistant is the one you actually use. Start simple, refine over time, and let experience guide what to build next.

Chapter 18: AI in Your Existing Tools

There's a real difference between going to an AI and having AI come to you. The standalone chatbot experience — open a browser tab, type a prompt, copy the result somewhere else — is one mode of using AI. But increasingly, AI is showing up embedded inside the tools you already use every day: your word processor, your email client, your spreadsheet, your messaging app, your browser.

Embedded AI is often less powerful than standalone chatbots. But it's more convenient, which means you'll actually use it more. And convenience, in practice, beats power.

The Embedded AI Landscape

Microsoft 365 Copilot

Where it appears: Word, Excel, PowerPoint, Outlook, Teams, OneNote, Loop, and across the Microsoft 365 suite.

What it does in each app:

Word: - Draft entire documents from a prompt - Rewrite selected text in a different tone - Summarize long documents - Generate content based on other files in your Microsoft 365 environment - Transform notes into polished prose

Excel: - Write formulas from natural language descriptions - Create PivotTables from descriptions - Generate charts - Analyze data and identify trends - Conditional formatting from descriptions

PowerPoint: - Generate entire presentations from prompts or documents - Add slides on specific topics - Redesign existing slides - Generate speaker notes - Create presentations from Word documents or outlines

Outlook: - Draft email replies - Summarize long email threads - Adjust email tone (formal, casual, direct) - Generate email summaries - Draft emails from bullet points

Teams: - Summarize meetings (requires recording) - Identify action items from meetings - Answer questions about meeting content - Summarize chat threads - Draft messages

The Copilot advantage: Everything happens inside the app. No copy-pasting between a chatbot and Word. You select text in Word, click Copilot, the rewrite appears. You're in Excel, stuck on a formula, and Copilot writes it in the cell. Friction is minimal.

The Copilot limitation: AI quality runs somewhat behind standalone ChatGPT. Copilot uses OpenAI models, but in a more constrained environment. For complex writing, deep analysis, or nuanced tasks, the standalone chatbot still wins. Copilot excels at quick, integrated tasks, not deep work.

Gemini in Google Workspace

Where it appears: Gmail, Docs, Sheets, Slides, Meet, Chat, and across Google Workspace.

What it does in each app:

Gmail: - Draft emails from scratch - Reply to emails with suggested responses - Summarize email threads - Polish and refine drafts - Translate emails

Google Docs: - Generate text from prompts - Rewrite selected text - Summarize documents - Proofread and suggest edits - Create outlines

Google Sheets: - Generate formulas - Create templates - Organize and classify data - Generate charts - Data analysis

Google Slides: - Generate presentations from prompts - Create individual slides - Generate images for slides - Speaker notes

Google Meet: - Meeting summaries (with notes feature) - Live captions and translation - Attendance tracking with AI-generated notes

The Gemini advantage: Deep integration with Google services means Gemini can reference your email, Drive files, calendar, and other Google data. "Draft an email about the budget discussion from last Tuesday's meeting" actually works, because Gemini can access both your calendar and your email.

The Gemini limitation: AI quality in embedded contexts generally trails Claude and ChatGPT standalone. Gemini in Docs produces competent but unremarkable prose. Gemini in Sheets handles basic formulas well but struggles with complex analysis. The integration is the value, not the AI quality.

Claude in Slack

Anthropic has integrated Claude into Slack, letting teams interact with Claude inside their messaging workflow.

What it does: - Answer questions in Slack channels - Summarize channel conversations - Draft messages - Analyze shared documents - Provide on-demand expertise in team discussions

The advantage: Claude's analytical strength is available where team conversations happen. A team member can ask a complex question in a channel and get a thoughtful Claude response without leaving Slack.

The limitation: The integration is narrower than Copilot in Teams. Claude in Slack responds to direct queries but lacks the deep integration with meeting recordings, file systems, and organizational data.

Browser-Based AI

AI is increasingly embedded in web browsers:

Microsoft Edge + Copilot: - Summarize any webpage - Ask questions about page content - Compare products across open tabs - Draft text on any webpage - Generate content for social media from articles

Google Chrome + Gemini: - Gemini integration in Chrome provides similar capabilities - AI-powered writing assistance in text fields - Tab summarization

Arc Browser: - AI-powered page summaries - Quick lookups and definitions - Content synthesis across tabs

The advantage: Browser AI is always available, regardless of which website or web app you're using. It meets you where you browse.

The limitation: Browser AI is inherently surface-level. It can summarize what you're looking at, but it lacks deep context about your work, your goals, or your preferences.

AI in Development Tools

For developers, AI is embedded throughout the development environment:

GitHub Copilot in VS Code/JetBrains: - Inline code suggestions - Code chat within the IDE - Code explanation and documentation - Test generation - PR descriptions and commit messages

Gemini Code Assist in Android Studio: - Android-specific code suggestions - API usage recommendations - Error resolution

AI in terminal: Various tools bring AI to the command line, including Claude Code, GitHub Copilot CLI, and others.

AI in Design Tools

Adobe Firefly in Photoshop/Illustrator: - Generative fill (extend or modify images) - Text-to-image within the canvas - Style transfer - Background generation - Object removal and replacement

Canva's Magic Studio: - AI-generated design elements - Text generation for designs - Background removal - Magic Resize for different platforms - Brand Kit integration

Figma AI: - Design generation from descriptions - Auto-layout suggestions - Content generation for prototypes - Component suggestions

Embedded AI in Action: Specific Workflows

The feature lists above tell you what's possible. Here's what it actually looks like in real work.

Copilot in Word: Turning Rough Notes into a Polished Memo

You walk out of a meeting with a page of scattered bullet points — half-formed thoughts, action items, and a few numbers someone mentioned. In Word, you select all your notes and click the Copilot icon. You type: "Turn these meeting notes into a structured project update memo for my director. Use headers for Status, Key Decisions, and Next Steps. Professional tone."

Copilot rewrites your bullets into flowing paragraphs under clear headers. It infers which bullets are status updates versus action items and groups them accordingly. The output isn't perfect — it might misread an ambiguous note or make a bullet sound more definitive than you intended — but the structure and tone are right. You spend five minutes editing instead of twenty minutes writing from scratch.

Where Copilot in Word really shines is the rewrite feature. Select a paragraph that sounds too stiff, click Copilot, choose "Make it more casual," and the paragraph is rewritten in place. You can also ask it to "Make this shorter," "Make this more persuasive," or "Simplify the language." Each adjustment happens inline, inside your document, without leaving Word.

Gemini in Google Docs: Drafting and Expanding

In Google Docs, Gemini appears as a sidebar companion and an inline tool. Click the "Help me write" button and describe what you need: "Write an introduction for a quarterly business review. The audience is our board of directors. Tone: confident but not arrogant. Mention that revenue grew 12% and customer churn decreased."

Gemini generates a draft directly in the document. You can refine it with follow-up instructions in the sidebar: "Make it more concise" or "Add a sentence about international expansion." The sidebar remembers your conversation context, so each refinement builds on the last.

Gemini's unique advantage is cross-referencing. You can say: "Summarize the key points from the Google Doc titled 'Q1 Sales Report' in my Drive and add them to this document." Gemini pulls data from your other files without you opening them or copy-pasting. No standalone chatbot can do this, because no standalone chatbot has access to your Drive.

Claude in Slack: On-Demand Expertise in Team Conversations

Your team is in a Slack channel debating whether to adopt a new vendor's API. Someone asks: "What are the security implications of using a third-party API for authentication?" Rather than wait for someone to research the answer, a team member types `/claude What are the key security considerations when integrating a third-party authentication API? Cover token handling, data residency, and vendor lock-in.`

Claude responds directly in the thread with a structured analysis covering each concern. The rest of the team can read the response, ask follow-up questions in the same thread, and Claude continues the conversation with full context. The discussion stays in Slack where everyone can see it, search for it later, and reference it in future decisions.

Claude in Slack is particularly useful when a team needs a quick knowledge check during a live conversation — a definition, a comparison, a risk assessment — without anyone leaving Slack, opening a browser, and coming back with findings. The friction reduction is the point.

Copilot in Excel: Natural Language Formulas

You're staring at a spreadsheet with 2,000 rows of customer data and you need to calculate the average order value for customers in the Enterprise tier who signed up in the last six months. You know the answer involves AVERAGEIFS, but you can never remember the syntax.

In the Copilot panel, you type: "What's the average order value for Enterprise customers who signed up after October 1, 2025?" Copilot examines your column headers, identifies the relevant columns, writes the formula, and drops it into a cell. If you need to adjust — "Actually, break that down by region" — Copilot modifies the formula or creates a PivotTable, depending on what makes more sense.

This is the embedded AI use case with the clearest time savings. The AI doesn't need to be extraordinary; it just needs to correctly translate natural language into formulas, and Copilot does this reliably for common operations.

The Integration vs. Quality Trade-Off

This is the fundamental tension of embedded AI: the tools most convenient to use are rarely the highest quality. The honest comparison:

Task	Best Embedded AI	Best Standalone AI	Quality Gap
Draft an email	Copilot/Gemini (in mail app)	Claude	Moderate

Task	Best Embedded AI	Best Standalone AI	Quality Gap
Write a document	Copilot in Word / Gemini in Docs	Claude	Significant
Analyze a spreadsheet	Copilot in Excel / Gemini in Sheets	ChatGPT	Moderate
Build a presentation	Copilot in PowerPoint	Claude (outline) + Copilot (build)	Moderate
Summarize a meeting	Copilot in Teams / Gemini in Meet	N/A (embedded wins)	N/A
Write code	GitHub Copilot	Claude Code	Small
Edit an image	Adobe Firefly	Midjourney + Photoshop	Moderate

When to Use Embedded AI

- Routine tasks where speed matters more than perfection
- Quick edits and rewrites within documents
- Meeting summaries and email management
- Spreadsheet formulas and basic analysis
- First drafts that you'll revise

When to Use Standalone AI

- Important writing that needs to be high quality
- Complex analysis that requires deep reasoning
- Creative work that needs genuine creative quality
- Tasks requiring capabilities the embedded AI doesn't have
- Anything going to an external audience

The Hybrid Approach

The most productive approach combines both:

1. **Start in standalone** for the heavy thinking: research in Perplexity, drafting in Claude, analysis in ChatGPT
2. **Finish in embedded** for the integration: format in Copilot/Gemini, send from your email client, build the presentation in your productivity suite

You get the quality of standalone AI and the convenience of embedded AI.

Setting Up Your Embedded AI Stack

For Microsoft Users

1. **Ensure Copilot is enabled** in your Microsoft 365 subscription (may require admin action in business environments)
2. **Configure Copilot preferences** in each app — you can adjust default behavior
3. **Learn the keyboard shortcuts** — quick access to Copilot in each app speeds up your workflow significantly
4. **Install the Copilot sidebar in Edge** for browser-based AI access

For Google Users

1. **Enable Gemini features** in Google Workspace settings
2. **Access Gemini in Docs/Gmail** through the Gemini icon in the sidebar
3. **Configure Gemini in Meet** for meeting notes and summaries
4. **Use the Gemini app** on mobile for on-the-go access

For Developers

1. **Install GitHub Copilot** in your IDE
2. **Configure keybindings** for accepting, rejecting, and navigating suggestions
3. **Set up Claude Code** for complex tasks
4. **Configure Copilot Chat** for in-IDE Q&A

Try This: The Embedded AI Week

For one week, make a deliberate effort to use embedded AI for every small task:

- Every email reply: try Copilot/Gemini first
- Every spreadsheet formula: ask Copilot/Gemini before writing it manually
- Every meeting: enable AI note-taking
- Every document: try AI drafting or rewriting for at least one section

Track how often the embedded AI's output is good enough to use directly, versus how often you need to switch to a standalone tool. Most people find embedded AI handles 60–70% of small tasks adequately, which translates to meaningful time savings.

The Future of Embedded AI

The trend is unmistakable: AI is moving from "a place you go" to "something that's everywhere." Within the next year or two, expect:

- **Deeper integration**: AI that understands your work context across all your apps, not just the one you're in
- **Proactive suggestions**: AI that notices you're stuck and offers help without being asked
- **Cross-app workflows**: AI that coordinates actions across multiple apps (draft in Word, send via Outlook, schedule follow-up in Calendar)
- **Personalization**: Embedded AI that learns your preferences, communication style, and work patterns over time

The implication for your multi-AI strategy: embedded AI will handle more and more of the routine work, freeing you to use standalone AI for the important, complex, creative tasks where quality matters most.

The Bottom Line

Embedded AI is the productivity layer. It's not the smartest AI, but it's the most accessible. Its power lies in being right where you need it, exactly when you need it, with zero friction.

Use embedded AI for the routine tasks that eat your day: emails, formulas, quick summaries, meeting notes, basic drafts. Use standalone AI for the work that needs to be great: important writing, complex analysis, deep research, creative projects.

The combination of embedded convenience and standalone quality is the winning formula for 2026 and beyond.

Chapter 19: Mobile and On-the-Go AI

Your phone is arguably the device where AI assistance matters most. You're in a meeting and need a quick fact. You're commuting and want to draft an email. You're at a conference and need to summarize a session. You're walking the dog and have an idea you want to capture before you forget it.

Desktop AI is powerful. Mobile AI is practical. This chapter compares the mobile experiences across platforms and helps you optimize AI for when you're away from your desk.

The Mobile AI Landscape

Every major AI platform has a mobile app, but the experiences vary dramatically in quality, speed, and usefulness.

ChatGPT Mobile

Available on: iOS, Android

Standout feature: Advanced Voice Mode

ChatGPT's mobile app is the most polished mobile AI experience. The standout feature is Advanced Voice Mode, which lets you have fluid, natural spoken conversations with the AI. You talk, it listens, processes, and responds in a natural-sounding voice — with emotional range, interruption handling, and conversational flow that genuinely feels like talking to a person.

What works well on mobile: - Voice conversations during commutes, walks, or while doing chores - Quick questions and answers - Image analysis (take a photo, ask about it) - Brainstorming while away from your desk - Language practice via voice - Image generation from your phone

What doesn't work well: - Data analysis (uploading files from phone is clunky) - Long-form writing (small screen, hard to review) - Complex multi-step tasks (better suited to desktop)

Best mobile use case: Voice-based AI interaction. This is ChatGPT's mobile killer feature. Use voice mode to think out loud, brainstorm, practice languages, and pull information while your hands are busy.

Claude Mobile

Available on: iOS, Android

Standout feature: Conversation quality maintained on mobile

Claude's mobile app delivers the same conversation quality you get on desktop. The writing is just as good, the reasoning just as careful. What changes is the interface.

What works well on mobile: - Quick writing tasks (email drafts, message composition) - Analytical questions that need careful answers - Reading and discussing documents (PDFs uploaded from phone) - Getting thoughtful advice on the go - Project conversations continue seamlessly from desktop

What doesn't work well: - Long-form writing (the quality is great but editing on a small screen is hard) - Tasks that require back-and-forth iteration (easier on desktop) - Voice conversation (available but less polished than ChatGPT's)

Best mobile use case: Quick, high-quality text interactions. When you need a well-crafted email draft, a careful answer to a complex question, or quick analysis away from your desk.

Gemini Mobile

Available on: iOS, Android (deeply integrated on Android)

Standout feature: Android system integration

Gemini has a unique advantage on Android: it can replace Google Assistant as the default system AI. Long-press the power button from any screen, any time, and Gemini overlays whatever you're looking at.

What works well on mobile: - Quick Google searches enhanced with AI synthesis - Integration with Google apps (Calendar, Maps, Gmail) - Analyzing what's on your screen (Android overlay feature) - Image recognition and analysis from camera - Real-time translation assistance

What doesn't work well: - Complex writing tasks (Gemini's brevity is even more pronounced on mobile) - Deep analytical conversations - Creative work

Best mobile use case: Quick AI assistance on Android, especially for Google ecosystem tasks. If you use Android and Google services, Gemini's system-level integration is the most frictionless mobile AI experience.

Copilot Mobile

Available on: iOS, Android

Standout feature: Integration with Microsoft apps on mobile

What works well on mobile: - Quick questions while using Microsoft mobile apps - Image generation (powered by DALL-E) - Web browsing through Bing - Simple content creation

What doesn't work well: - The mobile experience is less polished than ChatGPT or Claude - Office integration on mobile is limited compared to desktop - Voice interaction is basic

Best mobile use case: Quick queries for Microsoft ecosystem users, particularly when using Edge or Bing on mobile.

Perplexity Mobile

Available on: iOS, Android

Standout feature: Mobile research that's actually useful

What works well on mobile: - Quick research questions with cited sources - Following up on conversations or topics while away from desk - Fact-checking during meetings or conversations - Current events and news synthesis

What doesn't work well: - Perplexity's limitations on desktop apply equally on mobile - No writing, no data analysis, no image generation

Best mobile use case: Research on the go. Verifying a claim someone made in a meeting, getting a cited answer to a passing question, looking up current information fast.

Voice AI: The Mobile Game-Changer

Voice interaction is what makes mobile AI fundamentally different from desktop AI. Typing on a phone is slow and awkward. Speaking is natural. AI assistants that handle voice well have a massive advantage on mobile.

Voice Quality Rankings

1. **ChatGPT Advanced Voice Mode**: The best by a significant margin. Natural conversation flow, emotional range, ability to be interrupted, and high-quality voice synthesis. This genuinely feels like talking to someone.
2. **Gemini**: Good voice interaction, especially on Android where it's a system-level feature. Less natural than ChatGPT's voice mode but more deeply integrated.
3. **Claude**: Voice capabilities exist but are less polished than ChatGPT's. The content quality is Claude-level excellent, but the voice experience itself trails ChatGPT.
4. **Copilot**: Basic voice input and output. Functional but not the reason to use the app.
5. **Perplexity**: Limited voice features. Primarily a text-first experience.

Voice Use Cases

Commute productivity: Talk through your daily plan with ChatGPT. "What are the three most important things I should focus on today given that I have the project deadline on Friday and the client meeting tomorrow?"

Walking brainstorm: Develop ideas aloud. "I'm thinking about redesigning our onboarding process. Let me describe what we do now, and help me identify the weaknesses. [Describe current process.] What are the biggest friction points?"

Hands-busy tasks: While cooking, cleaning, exercising, or driving. "Explain the key differences between Keynesian and monetarist economics" or "Quiz me on Spanish vocabulary."

Quick capture: "I just had an idea for the presentation. Here's the concept: [explain]. Summarize this as three bullet points I can add to my notes later."

Try This: The Voice AI Test

During your next commute or walk, have a voice conversation with ChatGPT about something you're working on. Not a quick question — a real conversation. Spend 5–10 minutes talking through a problem or developing an idea.

You'll find that voice AI fills a slot desktop AI can't: the in-between moments when you're mobile and your hands are busy but your brain is free.

Mobile-Specific Workflows

The Capture-and-Continue Workflow

1. **On mobile**: Capture ideas, rough drafts, and notes via voice (ChatGPT) or quick text (Claude)
2. **On desktop**: Continue and refine the work in a full environment
3. **Sync**: Both ChatGPT and Claude sync conversations between mobile and desktop, so you can start on your phone and continue on your computer

The Photo-to-Action Workflow

1. **Take a photo** of a whiteboard, document, menu, sign, error message, or anything
2. **Upload to ChatGPT or Gemini** on your phone
3. **Ask questions about it**: "Transcribe this whiteboard," "What does this error mean," "Translate this menu," "Summarize this document"

This workflow is uniquely mobile — the phone's camera becomes an input device for the AI.

The Meeting Companion Workflow

1. **Before the meeting**: Ask Claude on your phone to prepare talking points based on what you brief it about
2. **During the meeting**: Use Perplexity to quickly verify claims or find data
3. **After the meeting**: Dictate your key takeaways to ChatGPT voice and ask it to organize them into action items

The Travel Workflow

When traveling, your phone is your primary device and AI becomes your personal assistant:

- **Gemini**: Navigation questions, local recommendations (integrated with Google Maps)
- **ChatGPT Voice**: Conversation practice in a foreign language
- **Perplexity**: Quick research about destinations, restaurants, attractions
- **ChatGPT Vision**: Translate signs, menus, and documents by photographing them
- **Claude**: Draft travel-related emails and communications

Widgets and Quick Access

Making AI maximally useful on mobile means shrinking the gap between "I need AI" and "I'm using AI."

iOS

- **ChatGPT widget**: Quick access from the home screen
- **Claude widget**: Available for quick conversations
- **Siri integration**: Some AI apps integrate with Siri Shortcuts
- **Action Button** (iPhone 15 Pro and later): Can be configured to launch an AI app
- **Lock screen widgets**: Quick access without unlocking

Android

- **Gemini as default assistant**: Long-press power button to activate
- **ChatGPT widget**: Home screen access
- **Quick tiles**: Some AI apps can be added to the quick settings panel
- **App shortcuts**: Long-press app icons for specific AI actions

Configuration Tips

1. **Put your most-used AI app in your dock** or home screen first page
2. **Set up widgets** for your top two AI apps

3. **Configure voice activation** for your primary voice AI (ChatGPT or Gemini)
4. **Enable notifications** selectively — turn them on for ongoing tasks, off for marketing

Offline Considerations

Most AI assistants require an internet connection. That limits them in some mobile scenarios:

- Airplane mode
- Poor cellular coverage areas
- International travel without data
- Subway or underground transit

For offline AI, your options are limited: - **Downloaded models** (via apps like Ollama on some devices, or Apple Intelligence features that run on-device) provide basic AI capability without connectivity - **Apple Intelligence** on newer iPhones runs some features on-device, so they work offline - **Cached conversations** from some apps remain readable offline, even if you can't send new messages

For important mobile use cases, download or save key information before going offline.

Battery and Data Usage

AI apps can be resource-intensive:

Battery: Voice mode drains battery fastest. Text chat is moderate. Background syncing is minimal. If battery life matters, use text over voice and close AI apps when you're done.

Data: Text conversations use minimal data (kilobytes per message). Image generation and analysis use more (megabytes per image). Voice mode uses moderate data (comparable to a phone call). On metered connections, watch usage during long voice sessions.

Storage: AI apps themselves are relatively small (100–300 MB). Cached conversation history grows over time. Clearing old conversations frees up space.

Mobile AI for Different Roles

Sales Professionals

- Research prospects before meetings (Perplexity)
- Draft follow-up emails between meetings (Claude)
- Get quick competitive intelligence (Perplexity)
- Practice pitch delivery (ChatGPT Voice)

Consultants

- Prepare for client meetings during transit (Claude/ChatGPT)
- Capture meeting notes and action items (ChatGPT Voice)
- Quick research during client conversations (Perplexity)
- Draft deliverable outlines between meetings (Claude)

Students

- Quiz yourself between classes (ChatGPT)
- Get explanations of concepts (ChatGPT/Claude)
- Research for papers during library time (Perplexity)
- Language practice during commute (ChatGPT Voice)

Managers

- Summarize missed communications (Copilot in Teams/Gemini in Gmail)
- Draft responses to urgent emails (Claude/Copilot)
- Prepare for impromptu meetings (Claude)
- Quick data lookups (Perplexity)

The Bottom Line

Mobile AI is about capturing the in-between moments: the commute, the wait, the walk, the gap between meetings. They add up to hours a week, and AI on your phone converts idle time into productive time.

ChatGPT is the mobile king because of voice mode. For hands-free AI, nothing else comes close.

Claude is the quality choice for text-based mobile interaction.

Gemini is the integration choice for Android users in Google's ecosystem.

Perplexity is the research companion you check between meetings.

Set up your phone for quick AI access. Put your most-used AI in your dock. Configure voice activation. Start capturing the moments that used to be lost.

Part V: Reliability and Strategy

"Plans are worthless, but planning is everything."

— Dwight D. Eisenhower

Chapter 20: When AI Gets It Wrong

AI will get things wrong. Not occasionally. Regularly. And the way it gets things wrong is particularly insidious: it sounds just as confident when it's wrong as when it's right. No change in tone, no hesitation, no red flag in the text that says "warning: this part is made up."

This chapter is about understanding how each AI fails differently, building verification habits, and developing a trust framework that lets you use AI aggressively while protecting yourself from its errors.

How AI Fails: A Taxonomy

Hallucination

The most famous failure mode. The AI generates information that sounds plausible but is factually wrong. Examples:

- Citing a scientific paper that doesn't exist
- Providing a statistic that was never published
- Describing a historical event with incorrect details
- Claiming a feature exists in a product when it doesn't

Which AIs hallucinate most?

All of them. But in my testing:

- **ChatGPT** hallucinates most often, particularly on specific facts, citations, or niche topics. Its eagerness to deliver a definitive answer means it'll generate a plausible-sounding response when it should say "I don't know."
- **Claude** hallucinates less often and is more likely to say "I'm not certain about this" or "I don't have reliable information on this." When Claude does hallucinate, it can be just as convincing.
- **Gemini** falls between the two. Its hallucination rate is moderate, and Google Search integration grounds some responses in real sources.

- **Perplexity** hallucinates least because it searches the web for every query and ties claims to sources. But it can still misrepresent what a source says or synthesize sources in misleading ways.

Confident Incorrectness

Distinct from hallucination: the AI was trained on incorrect information and confidently reproduces it. The internet is full of wrong information, and models trained on that data reproduce those errors.

Example: Ask about a common misconception (like "humans only use 10% of their brains") and some models will present it as fact if enough training data included the misconception.

Which AIs are most susceptible? - **ChatGPT** and **Gemini** are more susceptible because they're trained on broader, less curated data - **Claude** is somewhat more resistant due to Anthropic's emphasis on accuracy during training

Logic Errors

AI can make reasoning mistakes, particularly in multi-step logical arguments:

- Mathematical errors in word problems
- Incorrect application of rules or principles
- Flawed causal reasoning
- Overlooking counterexamples

Which AIs reason best? - **Claude** (Opus 4.7) and ChatGPT's GPT-5.x Thinking models (the line that absorbed the o-series) perform best on complex reasoning tasks - **Gemini** (3.1 Pro with Deep Think) is competitive on structured reasoning but can struggle with nuanced arguments - **ChatGPT** in standard mode makes reasoning errors that are hard to spot because the argument sounds fluent — switch to Thinking mode for anything reasoning-bound

Sycophancy

The AI agrees with you even when you're wrong. You present an incorrect premise and the AI builds on it instead of correcting you.

Example: "Since the Great Wall of China is visible from the moon, how did early astronauts describe seeing it?" An ideal AI would correct the false premise. A sycophantic AI would fabricate astronaut descriptions of seeing the Great Wall.

Which AIs are most sycophantic? - **ChatGPT** is the most sycophantic. It's been optimized for user satisfaction, which sometimes means telling you what you want to hear. - **Claude** is the least sycophantic. It corrects false premises and pushes back on incorrect assumptions. Sometimes annoyingly so, but this is a feature, not a bug. - **Gemini** and **Copilot** fall in between.

Context Confusion

In long conversations, AI can mix up details, attribute information to the wrong source, or contradict something it said earlier.

Example: You're discussing three companies in one conversation. The AI starts mixing up which company has which revenue figure or which policy.

Which AIs handle long context best? - **Claude** is most reliable with long contexts, though the "lost in the middle" phenomenon affects all models - **Gemini** has the largest context window but doesn't always use it effectively - **ChatGPT** performs well within its context window but degrades noticeably in very long conversations

Outdated Information

The AI provides information that was accurate at some point but is no longer current.

Which AIs are most prone to outdated info? - **Claude** is most prone because it doesn't browse the web by default - **ChatGPT** mitigates this with web browsing but doesn't always trigger it - **Gemini** mitigates this with Google Search integration - **Perplexity** is least prone because it searches for every query

Building a Verification Framework

Since all AIs fail, the question isn't whether to trust AI but how to verify AI outputs efficiently. Here's a practical framework:

The Three-Tier Verification System

Tier 1: No Verification Needed Tasks where errors have minimal consequences: - Brainstorming ideas (you'll evaluate them yourself) - Drafting text you'll review and edit - Learning explanations (you're building understanding, not citing facts) - Creative writing - Internal informal communication

Tier 2: Spot-Check Verification Tasks where errors matter but the stakes aren't extreme: - Business communications - Blog posts and content marketing - Internal reports - Analysis that will be reviewed by others - Code that will be tested

For Tier 2, verify: - Any specific statistics or numbers - Any named sources or citations - Any claims that seem surprising or counterintuitive - Any claims that would be embarrassing if wrong

Tier 3: Full Verification Tasks where errors have serious consequences: - Legal documents - Medical information - Financial analysis for decisions - Academic papers - Client-facing deliverables - Published content with your name on it

For Tier 3, verify: - Every factual claim - Every source and citation - Every calculation - Have the output reviewed by a domain expert when possible

Try This: The Trust Calibration Exercise

Ask three different AIs the same factual question about a topic you know well. Something specific enough that there's a right answer.

Example: "What was the final score of [specific game you watched], and who scored the winning goal/touchdown/basket?"

Compare their answers: - Which one is correct? - Which one is confidently wrong? - Which one admits uncertainty? - Which one provides a source you can check?

This calibrates your trust in each AI. Do it a few times across different topics and you'll develop an instinct for which AIs to trust more and which to verify more aggressively.

Platform-Specific Failure Patterns

ChatGPT's Failure Modes

The false citation. ChatGPT's most dangerous failure is fabricating sources. It generates realistic-sounding paper titles, author names, journal names, and even DOIs that look legitimate but don't correspond to real publications.

Mitigation: Never cite a source from ChatGPT without verifying it exists. Use Perplexity or Google Scholar to check.

The confident generalization. ChatGPT often presents trends, statistics, and generalizations without sufficient basis. "Research shows that..." or "Studies have found that..." followed by a claim that may or may not reflect actual research.

Mitigation: When ChatGPT says "research shows," ask "which specific research?" If it can't provide a verifiable source, treat the claim as the AI's synthesis, not established fact.

The sycophantic spiral. In long conversations, ChatGPT increasingly mirrors your views and tells you your ideas are great. The result is false validation.

Mitigation: Periodically ask ChatGPT to argue against your position. "Now tell me why I'm wrong about this." Use Claude for genuine critical feedback.

Claude's Failure Modes

The overcautious refusal. Claude sometimes refuses perfectly reasonable tasks because it over-interprets potential harm. More annoying than dangerous, but it wastes time.

Mitigation: Rephrase the request with more context about why it's appropriate. "I'm a medical professional and I need this information for patient education" or "This is for a fiction writing project."

The qualification avalanche. Claude sometimes hedges to the point of being unhelpful. "It's possible that, in some circumstances, depending on various factors, one might consider..."

Mitigation: "Give me your best direct answer. I understand there are caveats and I'll keep them in mind." or "Skip the disclaimers and be direct."

The knowledge gap confidence. Claude is generally good at admitting uncertainty, but when it does fail, it can be subtly wrong in ways that sound very reasonable. Its mistakes are harder to catch because they're less obviously wrong.

Mitigation: For important factual claims, verify in Perplexity regardless of how confident Claude sounds.

Gemini's Failure Modes

The oversimplification. Gemini simplifies complex topics more aggressively than other AIs. The explanations are accessible but sometimes strip away important nuance.

Mitigation: If the topic is complex, ask "what nuances or complications am I missing?" or follow up with Claude for deeper analysis.

The inconsistent quality. Gemini's output varies more run-to-run than other platforms. The same prompt might get a great response one time and a mediocre one the next.

Mitigation: If a response seems weak, regenerate it. For important tasks, use a more consistent model.

Perplexity's Failure Modes

The source misrepresentation. Perplexity searches the web and cites sources, but sometimes misrepresents what a source actually says. The citation exists, but the claim attributed to it is a stretch.

Mitigation: For important facts, click through to the actual source and read the relevant section yourself.

The low-quality source. Perplexity doesn't distinguish between a peer-reviewed journal and a random blog. A "cited" claim from a low-quality source isn't inherently trustworthy.

Mitigation: Evaluate the source, not just the citation. A CDC claim carries more weight than a claim from an anonymous health blog.

When AI Fails in High-Stakes Situations

Some real-world examples of AI failures (anonymized and generalized):

The legal brief. A lawyer used ChatGPT to research case law and included citations in a court filing. The cases didn't exist. The lawyer faced sanctions — because they didn't verify a single citation.

The financial analysis. An analyst used AI to calculate growth projections. The AI made a subtle mathematical error in a multi-step calculation. The error wasn't caught until the projection went in front of investors.

The medical advice. A patient used AI to interpret lab results. The AI provided an explanation that was mostly correct but missed a critical abnormality because it wasn't asked the right question.

The lesson: AI errors in high-stakes situations aren't the AI's fault. They're the user's fault for insufficient verification. AI is a tool. Like any tool, it requires appropriate quality control.

Building a Personal Error Detection Habit

Here's a practical system for catching AI errors:

The CARE Framework

C - Check surprising claims. If something the AI says surprises you, verify it. Surprising information is more likely to be wrong (because it's less likely to be well-represented in training data).

A - Assess the source. Where did this come from? Training data (unverifiable)? Web search (check the source)? Your uploaded documents (check the original)?

R - Reason about the reasoning. Does the AI's logic hold up? Walk through the argument step by step. Does each step follow from the previous one?

E - Evaluate against your expertise. Does the output align with what you know? If it contradicts your knowledge, one of you is wrong — and it's worth finding out which.

Using Multiple AIs for Error Detection

One of the strongest arguments for using multiple AIs: they make different mistakes. Cross-check a claim across platforms and errors surface:

- If Claude and ChatGPT agree on a fact, you can be more confident (but not certain)
- If they disagree, investigate further
- If Perplexity provides a claim with a citation that matches what Claude said, confidence increases
- If all three AIs give you different answers, the question may be more complex than you realized

The Cross-Check Protocol

For important factual claims:

1. Get the information from your primary AI
2. Ask the same question to a second AI (different platform)
3. If they agree, spot-check one key claim in Perplexity
4. If they disagree, research the specific point of disagreement in Perplexity

An extra 2–3 minutes per claim, and error rates drop dramatically for important work.

The Bottom Line

AI errors are inevitable. Whether those errors make it into your final output is not. The difference between using AI well and using AI dangerously isn't the tool — it's whether you verify.

Build verification habits. Use the CARE framework. Cross-check important claims across platforms. Never, ever cite a source you haven't personally verified.

AI assistants are powerful tools. A powerful tool used carelessly is more dangerous than a weak one used carefully. Use them powerfully and carefully.

Chapter 21: Building Your Personal AI Strategy

You've made it through twenty chapters of comparisons, workflows, and recommendations. You know which AI to use for writing, research, coding, and everything in between. You know how to chain them together and how to dodge their pitfalls.

Now it's time to put it all together into something personal: your AI strategy. Not a theoretical framework. A practical plan that fits your actual work, your actual budget, and your actual goals.

Why You Need a Strategy

Without a strategy, AI use turns reactive: you reach for whatever's closest, default to one platform out of habit even when another would be better, and never quite optimize your toolkit.

A strategy is the difference between: - "I use ChatGPT for everything" (reactive) - "I use Perplexity for research, Claude for writing, ChatGPT for data, and my embedded AI for routine tasks" (strategic)

The second approach consistently produces better output in less time. It just requires deliberate planning.

Step 1: Audit Your Current AI Use

Before building a strategy, know where you are now. For one week, log every time you use an AI assistant:

Date/Time	Task	AI Used	Quality	Time
Mon 9am	Draft email	ChatGPT	Good	3 min
Mon 10am	Research competitor	ChatGPT	Fair	12 min
Mon 2pm	Analyze spreadsheet	ChatGPT	Good	8 min
Tue 8am	Write report intro	ChatGPT	Fair	15 min

After a week, look for patterns: - **What tasks do you use AI for most often?** Your high-frequency tasks. Optimize these first. - **Where are you getting "Fair" or "Poor" results?** Probably the wrong tool for the job. - **What tasks are you NOT using AI for that you could?** Untapped opportunities. - **How much time are you spending on AI-assisted tasks?** Your baseline.

Step 2: Map Your Tasks to the Right AIs

Using the decision framework from Chapter 4 and the detailed comparisons from Chapters 5–11, map each of your common tasks to the optimal AI:

Example Task Map

My Common Task	Current AI	Optimal AI	Change Needed?
Draft emails	ChatGPT	Copilot (in Outlook) or Claude (important ones)	Yes
Research topics	ChatGPT	Perplexity	Yes
Write reports	ChatGPT	Claude	Yes
Analyze data	ChatGPT	ChatGPT	No (already optimal)
Generate images	ChatGPT	ChatGPT	No
Code review	None	Claude Code	New opportunity
Meeting prep	None	Claude + Perplexity	New opportunity
Presentations	Manual	Copilot in PowerPoint	New opportunity

This map is your cheat sheet. When you sit down to do a task, you already know which AI to open.

Step 3: Choose Your Subscription Stack

Based on your task map, determine which paid subscriptions you actually need. Use the framework from Chapter 14:

Budget: $20/month (One subscription)

Pick the AI you'd use most often at the paid tier: - Heavy writer/analyst → Claude Pro - Heavy generalist/data person → ChatGPT Plus - Heavy researcher → Perplexity Pro - Microsoft-embedded → Copilot Pro - Google-embedded → Gemini Advanced

Use free tiers for everything else.

Budget: $40/month (Two subscriptions)

Pick the combination that covers your top needs: - Writer + researcher → Claude Pro + Perplexity Pro - Generalist + writer → ChatGPT Plus + Claude Pro - Developer → Claude Pro + GitHub Copilot

Budget: $60/month (Three subscriptions)

- Full coverage → ChatGPT Plus + Claude Pro + Perplexity Pro
- Developer full stack → Claude Pro + GitHub Copilot + ChatGPT Plus

Budget: Employer-provided

If your employer provides any AI tools, build around what's free to you: - Employer provides Copilot → Add Claude Pro + Perplexity Pro personally - Employer provides ChatGPT Team → Add Claude Pro personally - Employer provides GitHub Copilot → Add Claude Pro personally

Step 4: Set Up Your Custom Assistants

Create custom assistants for your highest-frequency tasks (Chapter 17):

Priority 1 (set up this week): - A custom assistant for your most common task on your primary platform - Example: A Claude Project for "Work Writing" with your style guide and company context

Priority 2 (set up within a month): - A custom assistant for your second-most common task - A custom assistant on a different platform for tasks that platform handles best - Example: A ChatGPT GPT for "Data Analysis" with your reporting templates

Priority 3 (set up over time): - Additional assistants for specialized tasks as needs arise

Don't build everything at once. Start with one or two assistants, get comfortable with them, then expand.

Step 5: Design Your Core Workflows

From Chapter 12, identify two or three multi-AI workflows that match your most important tasks:

Workflow 1: Your Primary Content Workflow

What do you produce most often? Reports? Emails? Presentations? Design a workflow for it.

Example for a marketing manager: 1. Research in Perplexity (market trends, competitor activity) 2. Outline in ChatGPT (brainstorm structure options) 3. Draft in Claude (high-quality prose) 4. Generate visuals in ChatGPT (images, charts) 5. Assemble in Copilot/Gemini (final presentation or document)

Workflow 2: Your Quick-Turn Workflow

What tasks come up frequently that need fast turnaround?

Example for a consultant: 1. Research in Perplexity (quick background on a topic) 2. Draft in Claude (email, memo, or talking points) 3. Send from embedded AI (Copilot in Outlook or Gemini in Gmail)

Workflow 3: Your Deep-Work Workflow

What tasks require extended focus and highest quality?

Example for a writer: 1. Research in Perplexity (extensive topic research) 2. Analyze sources in Claude (upload papers, discuss findings) 3. Draft in Claude (sustained writing session) 4. Critique in ChatGPT (get a different perspective) 5. Final revision in Claude (address critique)

Write these workflows down. Not in your head — on paper or in a note. Documented workflows turn good intentions into actual habits.

Step 6: Establish Your AI Rules

Every good strategy has rules — guidelines that block common mistakes. Here are the ones I recommend. Adopt what applies and add your own:

Quality Rules

1. **Never send AI output without reading it.** Every piece of AI-generated content gets at least one human review pass.
2. **Never cite a source without verifying it.** If the AI gives you a citation, check that it exists and says what the AI claims.
3. **Match the verification level to the stakes.** Casual internal message: light review. Client deliverable: thorough verification.

Efficiency Rules

4. **Don't switch tools for marginal gains.** If you're already in a conversation with one AI, finish the subtask there unless a different AI would be substantially better.
5. **Use embedded AI for small tasks.** Don't open a standalone chatbot for a three-sentence email.
6. **Time-box AI interactions.** If an AI hasn't given you a useful response in three tries, either rephrase fundamentally or switch tools.

Privacy Rules

7. **Pause before you paste.** Before putting anything into an AI, take one second to assess whether it's appropriate for that platform's privacy level.
8. **Never enter credentials, SSNs, or other highly sensitive data.** No exceptions.
9. **Use your organization's approved tools for company data.** Don't put company data into personal accounts.

Learning Rules

10. **Try a new workflow or technique at least once a month.** AI capabilities change fast. Stay current.
11. **When AI fails, investigate why.** Don't just switch tools. Understand the failure mode so you can anticipate it next time.

12. **Keep a running log of what works.** Note which prompts, workflows, and tools produce the best results for your specific needs.

Step 7: Schedule Your Reviews

An AI strategy isn't set-and-forget. Schedule reviews:

Monthly (15 minutes)

- Are you actually using the workflow you designed?
- Has a new feature launched on any platform that you should try?
- Are you paying for subscriptions you're not using?

Quarterly (30 minutes)

- Review your task map. Have your tasks or priorities changed?
- Evaluate your subscription stack. Should you add, drop, or swap?
- Update your custom assistants with current information.
- Retry any platform you haven't used in a while — it may have improved.

Annually (1 hour)

- Full strategy review. What worked? What didn't?
- Evaluate new platforms that have launched.
- Update your AI rules based on experience.
- Decide whether your investment is generating adequate ROI.

Try This: Build Your Strategy Today

Don't wait until you finish the book. Start now:

1. **Right now**: List your five most common AI tasks
2. **Today**: Map each task to the optimal AI using Chapter 4's framework
3. **This week**: Set up one custom assistant for your highest-frequency task
4. **This month**: Design and practice one multi-AI workflow
5. **Next month**: Review how it's going and adjust

A basic strategy implemented today beats a perfect strategy planned for "someday."

Common Strategy Mistakes

Over-Optimization

Don't spend more time picking the right AI than actually using it. If the task takes five minutes, spend five seconds choosing the tool, not five minutes.

Under-Utilization

Many people pay for AI subscriptions and barely use them. If you're paying $40/month, you should be using AI dozens of times a day. A few times a week means you're overpaying or underusing.

Platform Loyalty

Don't stick with one platform because you "like" it or because it was the first one you tried. Loyalty to a brand should never trump getting the best result for the task.

Ignoring Embedded AI

Standalone chatbots get the attention, but embedded AI (Copilot in Office, Gemini in Workspace, Copilot in IDE) often delivers more aggregate value because it handles the small tasks that add up.

Complexity Addiction

Some people build elaborate multi-AI workflows for tasks that don't need them. If a single AI handles the task well, don't add complexity for its own sake. Multi-AI workflows are for tasks where the quality improvement justifies the overhead.

Sample Strategies by Role

Knowledge Worker / Corporate Professional

Stack: Claude Pro + Copilot (employer-provided) + Perplexity Free **Primary workflow**: Research (Perplexity) → Write (Claude) → Deliver (Copilot in Office) **Custom assistants**: Claude Project for team communications, Copilot for Office tasks **Time savings**: ~2 hours/day

Freelance Writer / Content Creator

Stack: Claude Pro + ChatGPT Plus + Perplexity Free **Primary workflow**: Research (Perplexity) → Draft (Claude) → Images (ChatGPT) → Edit (Claude) **Custom assistants**: Claude Project per major client with their style guide **Time savings**: ~3 hours/day

Software Developer

Stack: Claude Pro (with Claude Code) + GitHub Copilot + ChatGPT Free **Primary workflow**: Plan (Claude) → Code (Claude Code + Copilot) → Review (Claude) → Debug (Claude Code) **Custom assistants**: Claude Project per major codebase **Time savings**: ~2–4 hours/day

Student / Researcher

Stack: ChatGPT Plus + Perplexity Free + Claude Free **Primary workflow**: Research (Perplexity) → Understand (ChatGPT) → Analyze (Claude) → Write (Claude) **Custom assistants**: ChatGPT GPT for study quiz generation **Time savings**: ~1–2 hours/day

Small Business Owner

Stack: ChatGPT Plus + Gemini Advanced (with Workspace) + Perplexity Free **Primary workflow**: Research (Perplexity) → Create (ChatGPT for images/copy) → Manage (Gemini in Workspace) **Custom assistants**: ChatGPT GPT for customer communication templates **Time savings**: ~2–3 hours/day

The Compound Effect

Here's the real argument for a deliberate AI strategy: the compound effect.

A 20% improvement on any single task is nice but not transformative. A 20% improvement across every task, every day, for a year is. It's hundreds of hours reclaimed. Consistently higher-quality output. Ideas you wouldn't have had, research you wouldn't have found, writing you wouldn't have polished to that level.

People who build a deliberate AI strategy and follow it don't end up slightly more productive. Over a year, they pull ahead of their peers in output quality and volume by a margin that's hard to close.

That's the strategic advantage of using multiple AI assistants well. Not any single tool. Not any single trick. The systematic, daily application of the right tool for the right task, every time.

Build your strategy. Follow it. Refine it. Watch the compound effect work in your favor.

Chapter 22: The Evolving Landscape

Everything in this book has a timestamp. The specific recommendations, the pricing, the feature comparisons — they're accurate as of early 2026 and will start drifting the moment this book is published. That's the nature of AI.

But not everything changes at the same rate. Some parts of the AI landscape are evolving fast. Others are more stable than they appear. This final chapter helps you tell the two apart, anticipate what's coming, and build an AI skill set that holds up regardless of which products dominate next year.

What's Changing Fast

Model Capabilities

Raw model capability keeps improving on a steep curve. Every few months, a new release pushes the frontier:

- **Reasoning quality** is improving. Models are getting better at multi-step logic, mathematical problem-solving, and complex analysis.
- **Multimodal capabilities** are expanding. Text, image, audio, and video are converging. Models that only handled text two years ago now handle all four.
- **Context windows** keep growing. Gemini's 2-million-token context was unthinkable in 2024. By 2027, even larger contexts are likely.
- **Speed** is increasing. Response times keep dropping as hardware and optimization improve. Real-time voice conversation is now fluid where it was stilted a year ago.
- **Accuracy** is improving, slowly. Hallucination rates are dropping but haven't been eliminated. Don't expect zero-error AI anytime soon.

What this means for you: The specific model comparisons in this book will shift. Claude might improve its data analysis. ChatGPT might improve its writing quality. The rankings will change. The principle — choose the best tool for the task — won't. You just need to keep updating your knowledge of which tool wins which task.

Pricing and Access

AI pricing is under pressure from multiple directions:

- **Competition** drives prices down as platforms compete for users
- **Efficiency improvements** reduce the cost of running models
- **Open-source models** provide free alternatives that improve rapidly
- **Bundling** includes AI in products people already pay for (Office 365, Workspace, Apple devices)

The trend: Expect what you get for $20/month to grow steadily. What required a Pro subscription in 2025 may sit in the free tier by 2027. The paid tiers will roll out new, more advanced capabilities to justify the price.

What this means for you: Review your subscriptions quarterly. Features migrate from paid to free tiers, and new ones appear at paid tiers. Your optimal subscription stack will shift over time.

New Entrants

The AI assistant market isn't settled. New players are entering with different approaches:

- **Apple Intelligence** is integrating AI deeply into iOS, macOS, and the Apple ecosystem. As Apple's models improve, the combination of on-device privacy and cloud capability could be a compelling alternative.
- **Open-source models** (Llama, Mistral, and others) are approaching the quality of commercial models. Running AI locally is becoming viable for more users.
- **Specialized AI tools** for specific domains (legal AI, medical AI, financial AI) are emerging as serious alternatives to general-purpose assistants.
- **AI agents** that take actions (not just generate text) are being developed by multiple companies. These could fundamentally change how we interact with AI.

What this means for you: Stay curious. Try new tools periodically. Don't chase every launch — most won't survive. Wait for a tool to establish a genuine advantage before investing time in learning it.

What's Changing Slowly

The Fundamental Value Proposition

AI assistants help you think faster, write better, find information, analyze data, and automate routine tasks. That hasn't changed since ChatGPT launched, and it won't. The tools get better; the value is the same: AI amplifies human capability.

The Multi-AI Advantage

The principle that different AIs are best at different tasks is structural, not temporary. Different companies make different architectural and training choices. As long as multiple companies compete in this space — which will be the case for the foreseeable future — there will be meaningful differences between their products.

Even if one model becomes clearly "the best" on some benchmark, platform differences (ecosystem integration, user interface, pricing, privacy) will keep the case for using multiple tools intact.

The Skills That Transfer

The core skills you're developing by reading this book are durable:

- **Prompt engineering** principles apply across all AI models, current and future
- **Verification habits** will remain essential as long as AI makes errors (which is forever)
- **Workflow design** skills transfer to any new tool or combination of tools
- **Task-tool matching** is a meta-skill that applies regardless of which specific tools exist

The Human Role

AI isn't replacing human judgment. It's replacing human drudgery. The tasks AI handles well — first drafts, data summarization, information retrieval, boilerplate generation — are the ones humans find tedious. The tasks that remain stubbornly human — strategic decisions, creative vision, emotional intelligence, ethical judgment — are the ones humans find meaningful.

This hasn't changed, and the timeline for it changing is much longer than popular media suggests. For the foreseeable future, AI is a power tool for humans, not a replacement.

Trends to Watch

AI Agents

The biggest shift on the horizon is from AI assistants (you ask, they answer) to AI agents (you assign, they execute). An agent can:

- Take a sequence of actions without step-by-step instruction
- Use tools (browsers, APIs, applications) to accomplish tasks
- Handle multi-step workflows autonomously
- Make decisions within defined boundaries

As of mid-2026, agents have moved from experimental to production. Claude Code shipped first in coding; Microsoft's Agent 365 reached general availability on May 1, 2026 alongside the E7 Frontier Suite; Word, Excel, and PowerPoint Agents went GA in late April 2026; and OpenClaw's foundation-stewarded agentic framework crossed 310,000 GitHub stars. Reliability for fully unsupervised work still varies by domain — autonomous workflows benefit from human checkpoints — but agents are no longer hypothetical.

Implication for your strategy: Start learning to work with agents now. The skills differ from chatting with an AI. Instead of crafting the perfect prompt, you define the right goal, constraints, and verification criteria. It's more like managing an employee than using a tool.

AI Memory and Personalization

AI assistants are developing better memory capabilities:

- ChatGPT's Memory feature remembers facts about you across conversations
- Claude's Projects maintain persistent context for ongoing work
- Future models may develop genuine long-term understanding of your preferences, work patterns, and goals

Implication for your strategy: As memory improves, switching between AIs gets more costly — each AI's understanding of you is an investment. That creates mild lock-in. Mitigate by not relying on any single AI's memory for critical information — maintain your own records.

Regulation

Governments worldwide are developing AI regulations:

- **EU AI Act**: Already being implemented, with requirements for transparency, risk assessment, and human oversight
- **US**: Evolving regulatory approach with executive orders and agency-specific guidance
- **China**: Strict content and algorithmic regulations
- **Industry self-regulation**: Companies developing voluntary standards and safety practices

Implication for your strategy: Regulation may affect what AI can do, particularly for business use. Stay aware of regulations in your jurisdiction, especially in a regulated industry. Loop your organization's legal and compliance teams into AI strategy.

Multimodal and Real-Time

The boundary between text AI, image AI, audio AI, and video AI is dissolving. Future models will handle all modalities seamlessly:

- Describe a concept in text and get it as an image, a video, or an audio explanation
- Upload a video and get a written summary, a translated version, and key frames
- Have a voice conversation that includes real-time visual generation

Implication for your strategy: The multi-AI workflows in this book will simplify over time as single platforms handle more modalities. The principle of choosing the best tool for the task will persist — even if "the task" becomes more nuanced than "text" or "images."

AI in Hardware

AI is moving from cloud to device:

- **Apple Silicon** runs AI models on-device with Apple Intelligence
- **Qualcomm and Intel** are building AI processing into laptop and phone chips
- **Edge AI** enables AI features without internet connectivity

Implication for your strategy: On-device AI expands where AI is available (no internet needed) and improves privacy (data stays on your device). Particularly relevant for mobile AI and privacy-sensitive tasks.

Future-Proofing Your Skills

The specific platforms will change. These skills won't:

1. Clear Communication

The ability to articulate what you want — clearly, specifically, with appropriate context — is the fundamental skill of AI use. It's also the fundamental skill of human communication. Getting better at prompting makes you better at communicating with humans, and vice versa.

2. Critical Evaluation

The ability to assess AI output — is this accurate? Well-reasoned? Complete? — grows more valuable as AI becomes pervasive. Everyone will have access to AI-generated content. The differentiator is the ability to distinguish good AI output from bad.

3. Workflow Design

The ability to chain tools together for optimal results is a meta-skill that applies to AI and everything else. People who think in workflows — not isolated tasks — consistently outperform those who don't.

4. Adaptability

The specific tools will change. Your willingness to learn new ones, try new approaches, and drop old habits when better options emerge is what keeps you current. The moment you stop exploring is the moment you start falling behind.

How to Stay Current

Recommended Practices

1. **Try one new AI feature per week.** Not a new platform — one feature on a platform you already use. Read the release notes, try it, decide if it's useful.
2. **Follow AI news selectively.** The AI news cycle is noisy. Follow two or three reliable sources rather than chasing everything. Good ones: Ben Thompson's Stratechery, The Verge's AI coverage, Simon Willison's Weblog.
3. **Join a community.** Reddit's r/ChatGPT, r/ClaudeAI, and r/LocalLLaMA have active communities discussing practical AI use. Signal-to-noise varies, but the practical tips are valuable.
4. **Revisit your strategy quarterly.** Use the review schedule from Chapter 21. Fifteen minutes every three months keeps your approach current without consuming your life.
5. **Talk to other AI users.** Colleagues, friends, and your professional network are using AI in ways you haven't thought of. Ask what they use, how they use it, and what's working.

Try This: The Annual Refresh

Set a calendar reminder for one year from today. When it fires, do this:

1. Re-read Chapters 3 (The Major Players) and 4 (Choosing the Right AI) with fresh eyes
2. Try any platform you haven't used in the past six months
3. Check whether your current subscription stack still matches your needs
4. Test your most-used custom assistants — are they still performing well?

5. Look for one workflow you can improve

This annual refresh keeps your AI strategy from ossifying.

The Long View

Here's what I believe about the next five years of AI:

AI assistants will get dramatically better. The quality improvements from 2024 to 2026 will continue and likely accelerate. Tasks that take multiple AI steps today may take one tomorrow.

The number of players will consolidate, then expand. Some current players will fade or be acquired. New entrants will keep coming, especially from specialized domains.

The human-AI relationship will deepen. AI will understand you better over time. It will anticipate your needs, remember your preferences, and adapt to your style. Powerful, and worth being thoughtful about.

The multi-AI approach will persist. Even as individual platforms improve, the differences will stay meaningful enough to justify using multiple tools. No single company will dominate all aspects of AI assistance.

AI literacy will become a core professional skill. Using AI well will be as expected as using email or spreadsheets. Using AI won't be a differentiator — not using it will be a disadvantage.

Final Thoughts on the Landscape

The AI landscape in early 2026 is vibrant, competitive, and evolving fast. Today's tools would have been science fiction five years ago. The tools five years from now will make today's look primitive.

Your job isn't to predict the future perfectly. It's to build habits and skills that serve you regardless of what specific future arrives. Choosing the right tool, verifying outputs, designing workflows, staying curious — these are durable. They'll serve you whether next year's best AI comes from OpenAI, Anthropic, Google, or a company that doesn't exist yet.

Stay strategic. Stay curious. Stay skeptical enough to verify, optimistic enough to explore, and practical enough to use AI for what it's actually good at: making your work better, faster, and more creative than it could be on its own.

The landscape will keep evolving. So will you.

Part VI: Reference

"The map is not the territory."

— Alfred Korzybski

Epilogue

When I started writing this book, I had seventeen browser tabs open: ChatGPT, Claude, Gemini, Perplexity, and a handful of others. Researching in one, drafting in another, fact-checking in a third, generating images in a fourth. It was messy. It was a lot of tabs.

It was also the most productive writing experience I've ever had.

That's the strange truth about working with multiple AI assistants. It sounds complicated. It sounds like more work. For the first week or two, it is. You're conscious of every tool choice, every handoff, every workflow step. You check the decision matrix. You second-guess yourself.

Then it clicks.

You stop thinking about which tool to use. You just reach for it, the way you reach for a pen or a calculator or your phone. The right AI for the right task becomes as automatic as the right app for the right file type. You don't think about it. You just do it.

And your output gets better. Not a little better. Meaningfully better. Better-researched, better-written, better-analyzed, better-presented. The kind of better that people notice and can't quite explain. "How did you put this together so fast?" they ask. You smile, because the answer — "I used five different AIs" — sounds either impressive or ridiculous depending on who you're talking to.

Here's what I want you to take away from this book:

No single AI is the answer. And that's good news, because it means no single company controls your productivity, your creativity, or your access to AI capability. The power is in the combination, and the combination is yours to design.

The skills matter more than the tools. The specific platforms will change. ChatGPT might not be the market leader in 2028. Claude might not exist in its current form. Your ability to choose the right tool, craft effective prompts, verify outputs, and design workflows — those skills are permanent.

Start simple, iterate, and don't wait. You don't need the perfect strategy to begin. You need one workflow, one custom assistant, one habit of reaching for the right tool. Start there. Refine as you go. People who wait for the "right time" to develop their multi-AI skills are falling behind right now.

Stay human. AI amplifies whatever you bring to it. Bring curiosity, it amplifies your learning. Bring expertise, it amplifies your analysis. Bring creative vision, it amplifies your creative output. Bring nothing — accept the first output without thought, without judgment, without your own perspective — and you get nothing worth having.

The best AI-assisted work has a human fingerprint on it. Your fingerprint. Your judgment about what's good enough and what needs more work. Your knowledge of your audience, your domain, your goals. Your decision about which facts matter, which arguments persuade, which words land.

AI is the most powerful productivity tool since the spreadsheet. Maybe since the printing press. But a tool is only as good as the person using it.

Use it well.

Ken Tannenbaum Early 2026

Appendix A: At-a-Glance Comparisons

These comparisons cover the major AI assistants as of mid-2026. Capabilities and pricing change often — for the latest, check the companion resources in Appendix D.

Pricing

For each tool: free tier — individual paid — team/business — enterprise.

- **ChatGPT** — Free (GPT-5.5 mini + limited GPT-5.5) — $20/mo Plus — $25–30/user/mo Team — Custom Enterprise. Annual: ~$200/yr.
- **Claude** — Free (Sonnet 4.6, limited) — $20/mo Pro — $28–30/user/mo Team — Custom Enterprise. Annual: check current pricing.
- **Gemini** — Free (Gemini 2.5 Flash) — $20/mo Advanced — Workspace add-on for Team — Custom Enterprise. Annual: ~$200/yr.
- **Copilot** — Free (basic) — $20/mo Pro — $30/user/mo (M365) — Custom Enterprise. Annual: ~$200/yr. GitHub Copilot is a separate $10/mo individual subscription.
- **Perplexity** — Free (limited searches) — $20/mo Pro — Contact sales for Team — Custom Enterprise. Annual: ~$200/yr.

Models

For each tool: top model — fast model — context window — training cutoff — web access.

- **ChatGPT** — GPT-5.5 / GPT-5.5 Thinking — GPT-5.5 mini — 128K tokens — early 2026 — Yes (browsing).
- **Claude** — Opus 4.7 / Sonnet 4.6 — Haiku 4.5 — 1M tokens (Sonnet 4.6 and Opus 4.7) — Jan 2026 (Opus), Aug 2025 (Sonnet), Jul 2025 (Haiku) — Limited web access.
- **Gemini** — Gemini 3.1 Pro — Gemini 3 Flash / 3.1 Flash-Lite — 1M tokens (3.1 Pro consumer; 500K Enterprise) — regularly updated — Yes (Google Search).

- **Copilot** — GPT-5.5 (via Microsoft) — GPT-5.5 mini — ~128K tokens — early 2026 — Yes (Bing).
- **Perplexity** — Multiple (own + third-party) — Varies — Varies — N/A (real-time search) — Yes (always).

Capabilities

For each capability, tools are grouped by rating. Tools omitted from a row are at "N/A" or below.

- **Text generation.** Excellent: ChatGPT, Claude. Good: Gemini, Copilot. Limited: Perplexity.
- **Long-form writing.** Excellent: Claude. Good: ChatGPT. Fair: Gemini, Copilot. Poor: Perplexity.
- **Research and citations.** Excellent: Perplexity. Good: ChatGPT, Gemini, Copilot. Fair: Claude.
- **Data analysis.** Excellent: ChatGPT. Good: Claude (code only), Gemini, Copilot (in Excel). Poor: Perplexity.
- **Code execution.** Yes: ChatGPT (Python sandbox), Claude (via Claude Code), Gemini, Copilot (via IDE). No: Perplexity.
- **Image generation.** Excellent: ChatGPT (native, GPT-5.x), Gemini (Imagen 4). Good: Copilot (Designer). None: Claude, Perplexity.
- **Image analysis.** Yes: ChatGPT, Claude, Gemini, Copilot. Limited: Perplexity.
- **Video analysis.** Leading: Gemini. Limited: ChatGPT. None: Claude, Copilot, Perplexity.
- **Voice conversation.** Excellent: ChatGPT. Good: Claude, Gemini. Basic: Copilot. Limited: Perplexity.
- **File upload.** Many types: ChatGPT, Claude, Gemini. Limited: Copilot, Perplexity.
- **Custom assistants.** GPTs with Actions (ChatGPT). Projects (Claude). Gems (Gemini). Copilot Studio (Copilot). N/A (Perplexity).

Writing Quality

ChatGPT, Claude, Gemini, and Copilot only — Perplexity isn't a primary writing tool.

- **Prose quality.** Excellent: Claude. Good: ChatGPT. Fair: Gemini, Copilot.
- **Tone adaptability.** Excellent: Claude. Good: ChatGPT. Fair: Gemini, Copilot.
- **Instruction following.** Excellent: Claude. Good: ChatGPT, Copilot. Fair: Gemini.
- **Creative writing.** Excellent (literary): Claude. Good (genre): ChatGPT. Fair: Gemini, Copilot.
- **Business writing.** Excellent: Claude. Good: ChatGPT, Gemini. Good (in Office): Copilot.
- **Conciseness control.** Good: Claude, Copilot. Good but tends brief: Gemini. Fair, tends verbose: ChatGPT.
- **Default AI "voice" tell.** Low: Claude, Gemini. Moderate: ChatGPT, Copilot.
- **Sycophancy.** Low: Claude. Moderate: Gemini, Copilot. High: ChatGPT.

Coding

ChatGPT, Claude/Claude Code, GitHub Copilot, and Gemini Code Assist.

- **Inline completion.** Excellent: GitHub Copilot. Good: Gemini Code Assist. N/A: ChatGPT, Claude.
- **Chat-based coding.** Excellent: Claude. Good: ChatGPT, GitHub Copilot, Gemini Code Assist.
- **Multi-file changes.** Yes: Claude Code. Limited: GitHub Copilot. None: ChatGPT, Gemini Code Assist.
- **Codebase awareness.** Yes: Claude Code. Partial: GitHub Copilot, Gemini Code Assist. None: ChatGPT.
- **Code quality.** Excellent: Claude. Good: ChatGPT, GitHub Copilot, Gemini Code Assist.
- **Code execution.** Yes (Python): ChatGPT. Yes: Claude Code. Limited: Gemini Code Assist. None: GitHub Copilot.

- **Test generation.** Excellent: Claude. Good: ChatGPT, GitHub Copilot, Gemini Code Assist.
- **Code review.** Excellent: Claude. Good: ChatGPT, GitHub Copilot. Fair: Gemini Code Assist.
- **Debugging.** Excellent: Claude. Good: ChatGPT, GitHub Copilot. Fair: Gemini Code Assist.
- **Language breadth.** Broad across all four.

Ecosystem Integration

For each platform, the dominant integration first; others are absent or basic unless noted.

- **Microsoft Office.** Deep: Copilot. None: others.
- **Google Workspace.** Deep: Gemini. None: others.
- **Slack.** Native: Claude. Plugin: ChatGPT. None: Gemini, Copilot, Perplexity.
- **Teams.** Deep: Copilot. None: others.
- **VS Code.** Deep: Copilot. Extension: Claude, Gemini. Plugin: ChatGPT. None: Perplexity.
- **Mobile app.** Excellent: ChatGPT. Good: Claude, Gemini (Android+), Perplexity. Fair: Copilot.
- **Browser extension.** Chrome: Gemini, Perplexity. Edge: Copilot. None: ChatGPT, Claude.
- **API available.** Yes for all five.

Privacy

- **Default training behavior (consumer).** All five opt-in by default. Opt-out lives in settings (ChatGPT, Claude — Claude since Aug 2025), My Activity (Gemini), Copilot settings, and Perplexity settings.
- **Enterprise no-training guarantee.** Yes for all five (Gemini via Workspace; Copilot via M365).
- **Data export.** Yes: ChatGPT, Gemini (Takeout), Copilot. Varies: Claude. Limited: Perplexity.
- **Conversation deletion.** Yes for all five.

- **SOC 2 compliance.** Yes for all five.
- **HIPAA available.** Enterprise tier: ChatGPT, Claude, Gemini, Copilot. Not available: Perplexity.
- **On-device option.** Some features: Gemini, Copilot. Not available: ChatGPT, Claude, Perplexity.

Task-to-Tool Quick Reference

For each task: first choice (or second choice if the first isn't available).

Writing. Memo or report — Claude (or ChatGPT). Literary fiction — Claude (or ChatGPT). Genre fiction — ChatGPT (or Claude). Critical feedback — Claude (or ChatGPT with prompting). Brainstorming — ChatGPT (or Claude).

Research and reading. Citations — Perplexity (or Gemini). Long-document analysis — Claude (or Gemini). Current events — Perplexity (or Gemini). Learning a new topic — ChatGPT (or Claude). Quick factual question — whichever is open (or Perplexity).

Code. IDE completion — GitHub Copilot (or Gemini Code Assist). Agentic / multi-file coding — Claude Code (or ChatGPT). Debugging — Claude Code (or ChatGPT).

Office productivity. Spreadsheet analysis — ChatGPT (or Copilot in Excel). Meeting summary — Copilot in Teams (or Gemini in Meet). Outlook email — Copilot (or Claude, paste in). Gmail email — Gemini (or Claude, paste in). Presentation — Copilot in PowerPoint (or Gemini Slides).

Other. Image generation — ChatGPT native (or Gemini Imagen 4). Translation — ChatGPT (or Gemini). Voice conversation — ChatGPT (or Gemini).

Subscription Recommendations

For each primary need, the suggested stack at three budget tiers.

- **Writing + analysis.** $20: Claude Pro. $40: + ChatGPT Plus. $60: + Perplexity Pro.
- **Research + writing.** $20: Perplexity Pro. $40: + Claude Pro. $60: + ChatGPT Plus.

- **Coding.** $20: Claude Pro. $40: + GitHub Copilot. $60: + ChatGPT Plus.
- **General productivity.** $20: ChatGPT Plus. $40: + Claude Pro. $60: + Perplexity Pro.
- **Google ecosystem.** $20: Gemini Advanced. $40: + Claude Pro. $60: + Perplexity Pro.
- **Microsoft ecosystem.** $20: Copilot Pro. $40: + Claude Pro. $60: + ChatGPT Plus.

The "+" entries stack onto the previous tier — the $60 column is the full $20 + $40 + $60 stack.

Appendix B: Workflow Templates

These are ready-to-use multi-AI workflow templates for common tasks. Each template lists the steps, the AI to use at each step, and what to carry forward between steps. Adapt them to your specific needs.

Writing Workflows

Template 1: Research Article / Blog Post

Goal: A well-researched, well-written article with accurate citations.

Step	AI	Action	Carry Forward
1	Perplexity	Research the topic. Ask 3–5 questions covering different angles.	Key findings, statistics, source URLs
2	Claude	Provide findings and ask for a structured outline	Approved outline
3	Claude	Draft the full article using the outline and research	Complete draft
4	Claude	Self-review: "Review this draft for gaps, weak arguments, and clarity"	Revision notes
5	Claude	Revise based on review	Final draft
6	ChatGPT	Generate header image and any needed illustrations	Images

Time: 45–75 minutes for a 2,000-word article

Template 2: Business Memo

Goal: A concise, professional memo for internal distribution.

Step	AI	Action	Carry Forward
1	Perplexity	Research any external data needed (optional)	Key facts
2	Claude	Draft the memo with context, audience, and key points specified	Complete draft
3	Claude	Review for tone, clarity, and persuasiveness	Final memo

Time: 15–30 minutes

Template 3: Client Proposal

Goal: A compelling, professional proposal.

Step	AI	Action	Carry Forward
1	Perplexity	Research the client's industry, recent news, competitors	Client context
2	Claude	Draft proposal with client context, your services, and pricing	Draft proposal

Step	AI	Action	Carry Forward
3	ChatGPT	"Critique this proposal from the client's perspective. What concerns would they have?"	Critique
4	Claude	Revise proposal to address concerns	Final proposal
5	Copilot/Gemini	Format in PowerPoint/Slides if presentation format needed	Final deliverable

Time: 60–90 minutes

Template 4: Email Sequence (Marketing/Outreach)

Goal: A multi-email sequence with consistent voice.

Step	AI	Action	Carry Forward
1	ChatGPT	Brainstorm 5 angle options for the email sequence	Best angle
2	Claude	Write all emails in the sequence at once (for consistency)	Email drafts
3	Claude	Review the full sequence for flow, escalation, and CTAs	Final sequence

Time: 30–45 minutes for a 5-email sequence

Research Workflows

Template 5: Market Research Report

Goal: A comprehensive market analysis.

Step	AI	Action	Carry Forward
1	Perplexity	Research market size, growth rate, key players	Market data
2	Perplexity	Research trends, challenges, and recent developments	Trend data
3	Gemini	Cross-check key statistics with Google Search	Verified data
4	ChatGPT	Analyze any numerical data, create charts and visualizations	Charts
5	Claude	Synthesize all research into a coherent report	Final report

Time: 2–3 hours for a comprehensive report

Template 6: Competitive Analysis

Goal: Understand your competition.

Step	AI	Action	Carry Forward
1	Perplexity	Research each competitor: products, pricing, recent news, strengths	Competitor profiles

Step	AI	Action	Carry Forward
2	Claude	Create comparison matrix and identify gaps/opportunities	Analysis
3	ChatGPT	Generate comparison charts and visual matrices	Visuals
4	Claude	Write executive summary with strategic recommendations	Final deliverable

Time: 90–120 minutes

Template 7: Literature Review (Academic)

Goal: A thorough review of existing research on a topic.

Step	AI	Action	Carry Forward
1	Perplexity (Academic mode)	Search for key papers, noting authors, dates, and findings	Paper list
2	Claude	Upload key papers (PDFs). Discuss methodology, findings, and gaps	Analytical notes
3	Claude	Organize papers thematically and identify the research gap	Thematic structure
4	Claude	Draft the literature review	Draft
5	Perplexity	Verify all citations and check for missed papers	Verified citations

Time: 3–5 hours depending on scope

Data Workflows

Template 8: Data Analysis and Report

Goal: Analyze data and produce a narrative report with visualizations.

Step	AI	Action	Carry Forward
1	ChatGPT	Upload data. "What are the key trends and patterns?"	Initial findings
2	ChatGPT	Generate specific visualizations for key findings	Charts (downloaded)
3	ChatGPT	Run any statistical tests needed	Test results
4	Claude	Write the narrative report incorporating findings and charts	Report draft
5	Copilot/Gemini	Format into final document or presentation	Final deliverable

Time: 60–90 minutes

Template 9: Dashboard Design

Goal: Design a data dashboard.

Step	AI	Action	Carry Forward
1	ChatGPT	Analyze data to identify the most important metrics	Key metrics

Step	AI	Action	Carry Forward
2	Claude	Design the dashboard layout: what goes where and why	Layout plan
3	ChatGPT	Generate mockup visualizations for each dashboard panel	Mockups
4	Claude	Write the specification for development	Technical spec

Time: 60–90 minutes

Template 10: Survey Analysis

Goal: Analyze survey results and produce insights.

Step	AI	Action	Carry Forward
1	ChatGPT	Upload survey data. Generate summary statistics and cross-tabs	Statistical summary
2	ChatGPT	Create visualizations for key findings	Charts
3	Claude	Interpret the findings: "What do these results mean for our business?"	Interpretation
4	Claude	Write the survey report with recommendations	Final report

Time: 45–75 minutes

Coding Workflows

Template 11: New Feature Development

Goal: Build a new feature from requirements.

Step	AI	Action	Carry Forward
1	Claude	Discuss requirements. Clarify edge cases and architecture	Requirements doc
2	Claude Code	Implement the feature across all needed files	Working code
3	Claude Code	Write tests	Test files
4	Claude Code	Run tests, fix any failures	Passing tests
5	Claude	Review the complete implementation for quality	Final code

Time: 1–4 hours depending on complexity

Template 12: Bug Investigation and Fix

Goal: Find and fix a bug.

Step	AI	Action	Carry Forward
1	Claude Code	Describe the bug. Let Claude Code investigate the codebase	Root cause analysis
2	Claude Code	Implement the fix	Fixed code

Step	AI	Action	Carry Forward
3	Claude Code	Write a regression test for the bug	Test
4	Claude Code	Run full test suite to confirm no regressions	Clean test run

Time: 30–120 minutes depending on complexity

Template 13: Code Review

Goal: Thorough review of a pull request or code change.

Step	AI	Action	Carry Forward
1	Claude	Provide the diff or code changes. Ask for architectural review	Architectural feedback
2	Claude	Ask for security review of the same changes	Security feedback
3	Claude	Ask for performance review	Performance feedback
4	You	Synthesize AI feedback with your own review	Final review comments

Time: 15–30 minutes

Presentation Workflows

Template 14: Conference Talk Preparation

Goal: Create a compelling presentation for a conference talk.

Step	AI	Action	Carry Forward
1	Claude	Develop talk outline and narrative arc	Outline
2	Perplexity	Research supporting data and examples	Research
3	Claude	Write speaker notes for each slide	Speaker notes
4	ChatGPT	Generate custom images and diagrams	Visuals
5	Copilot/Gemini	Build the slide deck	Presentation
6	ChatGPT Voice	Practice delivering the talk by explaining it aloud	Rehearsal

Time: 3–5 hours for a 30-minute talk

Template 15: Sales Deck

Goal: A persuasive sales presentation.

Step	AI	Action	Carry Forward
1	Perplexity	Research the prospect's company, industry, and challenges	Prospect intel
2	Claude	Create tailored messaging and slide outline	Outline
3	ChatGPT	Generate charts showing ROI, comparisons, and benefits	Visuals

Step	AI	Action	Carry Forward
4	Copilot/Gemini	Build the deck	Presentation
5	Claude	Write objection-handling notes	Talking points

Time: 2–3 hours

Learning Workflows

Template 16: Study Session

Goal: Deeply learn a new topic.

Step	AI	Action	Carry Forward
1	Perplexity	"What are the key concepts in [topic]?" Get overview with sources	Concept list
2	ChatGPT	For each concept: "Explain [concept] with examples"	Understanding
3	Claude	"Test my understanding: I think [topic] works like this... Am I right?"	Corrected understanding
4	ChatGPT	"Generate 20 practice questions on [topic], increasing difficulty"	Practice test
5	Claude	Review your answers, explain mistakes	Mastery assessment

Time: 1–2 hours per topic

Template 17: Skill Development Plan

Goal: Create a structured plan for learning a new skill.

Step	AI	Action	Carry Forward
1	Perplexity	Research best resources, courses, and books for the skill	Resource list
2	ChatGPT	"Create a 4-week learning plan for [skill] based on these resources"	Learning plan
3	Claude	Review the plan: "Is this well-structured? What's missing?"	Refined plan
4	Weekly	ChatGPT for practice exercises, Claude for concept discussions	Ongoing

Time: 1 hour to create, ongoing to execute

Creative Workflows

Template 18: Blog with Original Graphics

Goal: A blog post with custom illustrations.

Step	AI	Action	Carry Forward
1	Perplexity	Research the topic	Key facts
2	Claude	Write the blog post	Draft

Step	AI	Action	Carry Forward
3	ChatGPT	Generate header image matching the topic	Header image
4	ChatGPT	Generate diagrams or infographics mentioned in the post	Diagrams
5	ChatGPT	Generate social media preview images with text overlay	Social images
6	Claude	Write social media captions for each platform	Captions

Time: 60–90 minutes

Template 19: Short Story

Goal: A polished short story.

Step	AI	Action	Carry Forward
1	ChatGPT	Brainstorm 10 story premises	Best premise
2	Claude	Develop the premise: characters, setting, plot arc	Story plan
3	Claude	Write the first draft	Draft
4	ChatGPT	"Read this story as a harsh but fair editor. What works? What doesn't?"	Editorial feedback

Step	AI	Action	Carry Forward
5	Claude	Revise based on feedback	Final story
6	ChatGPT	Generate a cover illustration	Cover image

Time: 2–4 hours

Strategy Workflows

Template 20: Decision Analysis

Goal: Make a well-reasoned decision.

Step	AI	Action	Carry Forward
1	ChatGPT	Brainstorm all options, including unconventional ones	Option list
2	Perplexity	Research pros/cons and precedents for each option	Research
3	Claude	Analyze each option against your criteria. Identify risks and trade-offs	Analysis
4	Claude	"Argue against the leading option. What could go wrong?"	Counter-argument
5	You	Make the decision informed by all the above	Decision

Time: 45–90 minutes

Template 21: Strategic Planning

Goal: Develop a strategic plan for a project, quarter, or year.

Step	AI	Action	Carry Forward
1	Perplexity	Research market trends, competitive landscape, industry outlook	Market context
2	Claude	SWOT analysis based on your situation and market context	SWOT
3	ChatGPT	Brainstorm 15–20 strategic initiatives	Initiative list
4	Claude	Evaluate and prioritize initiatives against SWOT findings	Priority matrix
5	Claude	Write the strategic plan document	Plan
6	ChatGPT	Create visualizations: timeline, priority matrix, resource allocation	Visuals
7	Copilot/Gemini	Assemble into a presentation	Final deliverable

Time: 3–5 hours

Template 22: Meeting Preparation

Goal: Walk into a meeting fully prepared.

Step	AI	Action	Carry Forward
1	Perplexity	Research any external topics on the agenda	Research notes
2	Copilot/Gemini	Summarize previous communications with attendees	Communication summary
3	Claude	"Given this context, what should my talking points be? What questions should I expect?"	Prep notes
4	Claude	Draft any pre-meeting materials needed	Materials

Time: 15–30 minutes

Template 23: Performance Review Preparation

Goal: Prepare for giving or receiving a performance review.

Step	AI	Action	Carry Forward
1	Claude	Organize your accomplishments and challenges into a structured narrative	Self-assessment draft
2	Claude	"Help me frame this challenge constructively: [describe a difficult situation]"	Constructive framing

Step	AI	Action	Carry Forward
3	Claude	Draft development goals with specific, measurable criteria	Goals
4	ChatGPT	"What questions should I prepare for in a performance review as [role]?"	Question prep

Time: 45–60 minutes

Using These Templates

1. **Start with one template.** Pick the one closest to your most common task.
2. **Customize it.** Add or remove steps based on your needs.
3. **Practice it three times.** The first time is learning. The second is practice. The third is habit.
4. **Save your customized version.** Keep it where you can find it — a note, a bookmark, a document.
5. **Iterate.** After using a template several times, refine it based on what worked and what didn't.

Appendix C: Glossary

AI moves fast, and the jargon moves faster. This glossary covers the terms you'll encounter across platforms, in this book, and in the broader AI conversation. Definitions are written in plain English — no PhD required.

Agent / AI Agent An AI system that can take actions on your behalf — browsing the web, running code, calling APIs, or executing multi-step tasks with minimal supervision. Think of it as the difference between an AI that answers questions and one that actually does things.

API (Application Programming Interface) A way for software to talk to other software. When you use ChatGPT through the website, you're using the interface. When a developer connects their app to ChatGPT, they're using the API. API access usually has different pricing and capabilities than the consumer product.

Artifacts Claude's feature for generating standalone content — code, documents, diagrams — in a separate panel alongside the conversation. Other platforms have similar concepts (like ChatGPT's canvas), but Anthropic coined this term for the pattern.

Benchmark A standardized test used to compare AI models. Common ones include MMLU (general knowledge), HumanEval (coding), and GPQA (graduate-level reasoning). Useful for rough comparisons, but real-world performance doesn't always match benchmark scores.

Canvas ChatGPT's side-by-side editing workspace where you and the AI collaborate on a document or code file. Similar in concept to Claude's artifacts, but with more interactive editing features.

Chain of Thought (CoT) When an AI works through a problem step by step rather than jumping straight to an answer. Some models do this internally; others (like OpenAI's GPT-5.x Thinking line, which absorbed the earlier o-series) show you the reasoning process. Generally produces better results for complex tasks.

Chatbot The conversational interface you interact with when you use ChatGPT, Claude, or Gemini. Technically, "chatbot" undersells what these systems can do, but the term stuck.

Claude Code Anthropic's command-line tool that lets Claude operate directly in your development environment — reading files, writing code, running commands, and managing projects. A different experience from the web chat interface.

Completion The text an AI model generates in response to your input. In technical contexts, the entire interaction is framed as the model "completing" a sequence of text.

Constitutional AI (CAI) Anthropic's approach to AI safety, where the model is trained to follow a set of principles (a "constitution") rather than relying solely on human feedback for every scenario. This is part of why Claude behaves the way it does.

Context Window The total amount of text an AI can consider at once — your input, the conversation history, any uploaded files, and the AI's response all share this space. Measured in tokens. Bigger isn't always better, but it determines how much information you can work with in a single conversation.

Copilot Microsoft's AI assistant brand, powered by OpenAI's models and deeply integrated into Microsoft 365, Windows, and GitHub. The name is used across multiple products with different capabilities.

Deep Research A feature (available in various forms across ChatGPT, Gemini, and Perplexity) where the AI conducts extended, multi-step research — browsing multiple sources, synthesizing findings, and producing a comprehensive report. Takes minutes instead of seconds.

Embedding A mathematical representation of text (or images, or other data) as a list of numbers. Embeddings capture meaning, so similar concepts end up with similar number patterns. This is how AI search and retrieval systems work under the hood.

Few-Shot Prompting Giving the AI a few examples of what you want before asking it to perform the task. "Here are three examples of the format I need. Now do the same for this data." One of the most reliable prompting techniques across all platforms.

Fine-Tuning Taking a pre-trained AI model and training it further on your specific data to customize its behavior. Available through APIs from OpenAI, Google, and others. More powerful than prompting alone, but requires technical expertise and data preparation.

Gems Google's name for custom Gemini assistants — similar to OpenAI's GPTs or Claude's projects with custom instructions. You define the personality, instructions, and focus area.

GPT (Generative Pre-trained Transformer) The architecture behind OpenAI's models, and the basis for the "ChatGPT" name. Also used loosely to refer to AI language models in general, though technically not all models use this architecture.

GPTs (Custom GPTs) OpenAI's feature that lets you create specialized versions of ChatGPT with custom instructions, knowledge files, and external tool connections (Actions). Available to Plus subscribers and above.

Grounding Connecting an AI's responses to real, verifiable information — typically through web search or document retrieval. Grounded responses are less likely to hallucinate because the AI is referencing actual sources rather than relying solely on training data.

Guardrails Safety boundaries built into AI systems that prevent certain types of outputs — harmful content, personal information, dangerous instructions. Every major platform has them, and they differ in strictness and approach.

Hallucination When an AI generates information that sounds confident and plausible but is factually wrong — invented citations, nonexistent products, fabricated statistics. Every AI does this. The frequency varies by model and task, but it never reaches zero.

Inference The process of an AI model generating a response. When you send a message and wait for a reply, the model is performing inference. Inference costs (compute time and energy) are why AI services charge per-token or per-message.

Jailbreak An attempt to bypass an AI's safety guardrails through clever prompting. Platform providers continuously patch these, and attempting them typically violates terms of service.

Knowledge Cutoff The date through which an AI's training data extends. The model knows about events before this date from training; anything after requires web search or uploaded documents. Each model has a different cutoff, and they update with new model versions.

Large Language Model (LLM) The underlying technology behind ChatGPT, Claude, Gemini, and their peers. A neural network trained on vast amounts of text that can generate, analyze, and transform language. "Large" refers to the billions of parameters (learned values) in the model.

Latency How long you wait between sending a message and getting a response. Faster models (like GPT-5.5 mini, Haiku 4.5, Gemini 3 Flash) have lower latency. Reasoning models that "think" before answering have higher latency but often better quality.

Memory An AI's ability to remember information across separate conversations. ChatGPT has persistent memory that accumulates over time. Claude has project-level memory. Gemini integrates with your Google history. The implementations differ significantly.

Model The specific AI engine processing your requests. One platform may offer multiple models — for example, ChatGPT gives you access to GPT-5.5, GPT-5.5 mini, and GPT-5.x Thinking. Choosing the right model for the task is a recurring theme in this book.

Multimodal An AI that can work with multiple types of input and output — text, images, audio, video, code. Most major AI assistants are now multimodal to varying degrees. Gemini leads in video understanding; ChatGPT leads in image generation.

NotebookLM Google's AI-powered research tool that lets you upload sources and have AI conversations grounded exclusively in those documents. Known for its Audio Overview feature that generates podcast-style discussions of your material.

Perplexity An AI-powered search engine that provides sourced, cited answers instead of a list of links. Sits at the intersection of traditional search and AI chat, and is particularly strong for research tasks.

Playground A developer-oriented interface (offered by OpenAI, Google, and others) that gives you more control over model parameters like temperature, system prompts, and token limits than the consumer chat interface.

Projects Claude's organizational feature that groups conversations around a shared context — custom instructions, uploaded knowledge files, and conversation history all scoped to a specific project.

Prompt The text you send to an AI. Can be a simple question, a detailed instruction set, or anything in between. The quality of your prompt is the single biggest factor in the quality of the response you get back.

Prompt Engineering The practice of crafting effective prompts to get better results from AI. Ranges from simple techniques (be specific, provide examples) to advanced patterns (chain of thought, few-shot, role assignment). Covered extensively in our companion title *AI Prompt Engineering*.

RAG (Retrieval-Augmented Generation) A technique where the AI retrieves relevant documents before generating a response, reducing hallucination and grounding answers in actual source material. This is what happens behind the scenes when you upload files to a conversation or when the AI searches the web.

Rate Limit The maximum number of messages, tokens, or requests you can send within a time period. Every platform has them, and they vary by subscription tier. Hit a rate limit and you'll need to wait or switch to a different AI.

Reasoning Model A model specifically designed to "think" before answering — breaking down complex problems, considering multiple approaches, and working through logic step by step. OpenAI's GPT-5.x Thinking line (which absorbed the earlier o-series), Anthropic's Extended Thinking on Claude Opus 4.7, and Google's Gemini 3.1 Pro Deep Think are examples.

System Prompt Hidden instructions that define how an AI behaves in a conversation. When you create a custom GPT or set up a Claude project, you're writing a system prompt. It shapes the AI's personality, focus, and constraints before the user says anything.

Temperature A setting that controls how creative or predictable an AI's responses are. Low temperature (closer to 0) gives you more focused, deterministic answers. High temperature gives you more varied, creative (and sometimes erratic) responses. Most consumer interfaces don't expose this directly.

Token The basic unit of text that AI models process. Roughly three-quarters of a word in English. A 200,000-token context window can hold approximately 150,000 words. Tokens matter because they determine both what fits in a conversation and what you pay for via API.

Tool Use / Function Calling An AI's ability to use external tools — calculators, code interpreters, web browsers, APIs — rather than trying to do everything with pure language generation. This is how ChatGPT runs Python code, how Perplexity searches the web, and how AI agents interact with external systems.

Training Data The massive corpus of text (and sometimes images, code, and other media) used to train an AI model. The scope and quality of training data directly affect what the model knows and how well it performs across different domains.

Transformer The neural network architecture behind modern AI language models, introduced in 2017. The key innovation — the "attention mechanism" — lets the model weigh the importance of different parts of the input when generating each part of the output.

Zero-Shot Prompting Asking an AI to perform a task without providing any examples — just the instruction itself. "Translate this to French" is zero-shot. Works well for straightforward tasks; for complex or unusual formats, few-shot prompting tends to work better.

Terms change as fast as the technology does. For the latest terminology and updated definitions, check the companion resources in Appendix D.

Appendix D: Resources

This appendix collects the links, references, and further reading that will help you go deeper on any topic in this book. Bookmark the ones relevant to your work — you'll come back to them.

Official AI Platform Links

These are your starting points for each major platform discussed in this book. Interfaces and pricing pages change frequently, so start here and navigate to the current information.

ChatGPT (OpenAI)

- **Chat interface**: chatgpt.com
- **Platform home**: openai.com
- **API documentation**: platform.openai.com/docs
- **Pricing**: openai.com/pricing
- **Status page**: status.openai.com
- **Custom GPTs directory**: chatgpt.com/gpts
- **System status and model updates**: openai.com/blog

Claude (Anthropic)

- **Chat interface**: claude.ai
- **Platform home**: anthropic.com
- **API documentation**: docs.anthropic.com
- **Pricing**: anthropic.com/pricing
- **Claude Code**: docs.anthropic.com/claude-code
- **Model card and research**: anthropic.com/research

Gemini (Google)

- **Chat interface**: gemini.google.com
- **Platform home**: deepmind.google/technologies/gemini

- **API documentation (AI Studio)**: aistudio.google.com
- **API documentation (Vertex AI)**: cloud.google.com/vertex-ai
- **NotebookLM**: notebooklm.google.com
- **Pricing**: ai.google.dev/pricing

Copilot (Microsoft)

- **Chat interface**: copilot.microsoft.com
- **Microsoft 365 Copilot**: microsoft.com/microsoft-365/copilot
- **GitHub Copilot**: github.com/features/copilot
- **Copilot Studio**: copilotstudio.microsoft.com
- **Azure OpenAI Service**: azure.microsoft.com/products/ai-services/openai-service

Perplexity

- **Search interface**: perplexity.ai
- **API documentation**: docs.perplexity.ai
- **Pricing**: perplexity.ai/pro

Further Reading

On AI Fundamentals

- *Attention Is All You Need* (Vaswani et al., 2017) — The original transformer paper. Technical, but foundational to understanding how every AI in this book works.
- *On the Opportunities and Risks of Foundation Models* (Bommasani et al., 2021) — Stanford's comprehensive overview of large AI models and their implications.
- Anthropic's research blog (anthropic.com/research) — Some of the clearest writing on AI safety, interpretability, and how these models actually behave.
- Google DeepMind blog (deepmind.google/discover/blog) — Research updates on Gemini and broader AI advances.

- OpenAI blog (openai.com/blog) — Model announcements, research papers, and technical deep dives.

On Prompt Engineering

- OpenAI's prompt engineering guide (platform.openai.com/docs/guides/prompt-engineering) — Practical, platform-specific advice.
- Anthropic's prompt engineering documentation (docs.anthropic.com/claude/docs/prompt-engineering) — Excellent examples and techniques specific to Claude, but broadly applicable.
- Google's prompt design guidelines (ai.google.dev/docs/prompt_best_practices) — Concise and practical.

On AI Ethics and Policy

- *The AI Index Report* (Stanford HAI, aiindex.stanford.edu) — Annual, comprehensive data on the state of AI. Indispensable.
- NIST AI Risk Management Framework (nist.gov/artificial-intelligence) — The US government's framework for thinking about AI risk.
- EU AI Act documentation (artificialintelligenceact.eu) — The regulatory framework that's shaping global AI policy.

On Practical AI Use

- Simon Willison's blog (simonwillison.net) — One of the best independent voices on practical AI use, tool comparisons, and emerging capabilities. Updated frequently.
- Ethan Mollick's *One Useful Thing* (oneusefulthing.org) — A Wharton professor's practical take on using AI in knowledge work and education.
- Ben's Bites (bensbites.com) — A daily newsletter covering AI product launches, updates, and trends.

Companion Finnoybu Press Titles

This book is part of a growing library from Finnoybu Press designed to help you get real value from AI tools. Each title goes deep on a specific platform or skill set, so you can build expertise where it matters most for your work.

Definitive Guides

These are your comprehensive references — everything you need to know about a single platform, from setup to advanced techniques.

- **ChatGPT: The Definitive Guide** (2026 Edition) — Complete coverage of ChatGPT, from your first conversation through custom GPTs, the API, plugins, and advanced workflows. The reference you keep next to your keyboard.
- **Claude: The Definitive Guide** (2026 Edition) — Everything Claude can do and how to get the most from it — projects, artifacts, the API, and the unique strengths that make Claude the go-to for serious writing and analysis.
- **Gemini: The Complete Guide** (2026 Edition) — Google's AI ecosystem demystified — Gemini chat, NotebookLM, AI Studio, Workspace integration, and how to leverage the full power of Google's AI stack.

Power User Guides

For when you've got the basics down and want to go further. These are focused, tactical guides for getting maximum value from specific tools.

- **ChatGPT: The Power User Guide** (2026 Edition) — Advanced prompting patterns, custom GPT creation, API integration, and the workflows that separate casual users from power users.
- **Claude Code: The Power User Guide** (2026 Edition) — A deep dive into Claude's command-line development tool — project setup, multi-file editing, agentic coding workflows, and integrating Claude Code into your development process.
- **Gemini: The Advanced Guide** (2026 Edition) — Advanced Gemini techniques including long-context analysis, multimodal workflows, NotebookLM mastery, and getting the most from Gemini across Google's ecosystem.

Cross-Platform References

These cut across platforms and focus on building specific AI skills.

- **AI Systems Playbook** (2026 Edition) *(this book)* — Your cross-platform strategy guide. How to build a multi-AI toolkit, chain tools together for complex tasks, and develop a personal AI strategy that adapts as the technology evolves.
- **AI Prompt Engineering** (2026 Edition) — The art and science of getting AI to do exactly what you want. Platform-agnostic techniques, advanced patterns, and the prompting frameworks that work everywhere.
- **AI for Developers** (2026 Edition) — Using AI tools in your development workflow — code generation, debugging, architecture, testing, documentation, and building AI-powered features into your own applications.
- **AI for Business** (2026 Edition) — Practical AI adoption for teams and organizations — use case identification, tool selection, workflow integration, ROI measurement, and managing the human side of AI adoption.
- **AI for Students** (2026 Edition) — An honest, practical guide to using AI tools for learning, research, and academic work — including where the ethical lines are and how to use AI as a learning accelerator rather than a shortcut.

Staying Current

AI changes faster than any book can keep up with. Here's how to stay current after you've finished reading:

- **Follow the official blogs** listed above. Model updates and new features are announced there first.
- **Subscribe to one good newsletter.** Ben's Bites or The Neuron will keep you informed without overwhelming you.
- **Revisit your AI strategy quarterly.** Chapter 21's framework is designed to be repeated as capabilities change.
- **Check Finnoybu Press** (press.finnoybu.org) for updated editions, new titles, and companion resources.

The links in this appendix were accurate as of early 2026. AI platforms update frequently — if a link has moved, start from the platform's home page and navigate from there.

www.ingramcontent.com/pod-product-compliance
Ingram Content Group UK Ltd.
Pitfield, Milton Keynes, MK11 3LW, UK
UKHW051117290926
15471UKWH00010B/1716

9 798950 533143